All designers will know how difficult
it is to find assistants who are intelligent, loyal
and good humoured. We did. And, in
appreciation, we dedicate this book to
Anna, Brian, George, Grant, Jessica and Sarah.

Graphic design: visual comparisons

by Alan Fletcher/Colin Forbes/Bob Gill

Studio Vista : London
Reinhold Publishing Corporation : New York

PUBLISHED IN LONDON BY STUDIO VISTA LTD,
BLUE STAR HOUSE, HIGHGATE HILL, N 19
AND IN NEW YORK BY REINHOLD PUBLISHING CORPORATION
430 PARK AVENUE, NEW YORK
SET IN 11/13 PT GARAMOND
REPRINTED 1964, 1966
LIBRARY OF CONGRESS CATALOG CARD NUMBER 64 - 14628
PRINTED IN THE NETHERLANDS
BY N.V. DRUKKERIJ KOCH & KNUTTEL, GOUDA

Introduction

We were asked to write a book on graphics, but unfortunately we are not writers. We felt we could best express our opinions with illustrations rather than theory.

The vast majority of advertisements, posters, television commercials, booklets and other printed matter clutter our environment and insult our intelligence.

And besides, they are so monumentally boring.

There are, however, some designers and even clients who insist that the public deserve and will respond to much higher standards in graphics. They are convinced, as Charlie Chaplin was convinced, that the best way to entertain the public is first to entertain oneself.

Our thesis is that any one visual problem has an infinite number of solutions; that many of them are valid; that solutions ought to derive from the subject matter; that the designer should therefore have no preconceived graphic style.

To demonstrate this we have selected a number of solutions to advertising and communication problems that are efficient and imaginative.

We have paired contrasting or complementary solutions to similar problems; we hope that these juxtapositions will stimulate students and professionals, if only to disagree with them.

Several considerations have limited our selection. Designs which required a large format, or used specific colour not available in this book, or those which were technically difficult to reproduce, had to be omitted. We also had to eliminate many brilliant examples for which we could not find an opposite number. With few exceptions we have chosen recent work so that this book will also reflect the climate of the sixties.

The credits, which are listed at the end of the book, presented a problem. One tends to give either too much or too little information in a project of this kind. We have given credits to the problem, to the individual or individuals who actually solved the problem, and to the client.

The designers represented in this collection do not belong to any one school. They work in America, France, Germany, Holland, Iceland, Italy, Poland, Sweden, Switzerland and the United Kingdom. They do have, however, some ideas in common.

Although most of them have done well in their profession, they believe that design is not a business but a way of life.

Unlike painters who *should* have a personal handwriting, designers are often anonymous, but their work still achieves a vived personality. Their identity is maintained by a consistently high standard of problem solving rather than by a consistent technique or style.

Of course there are always some impossible clients, but they know that the ultimate responsibility for a bad job rests with the designer and not with the client, however hardheaded and obstreperous. After all, they reason, there are many ways to solve a graphic problem. If one solution is rejected, another must be found.

Each job they do represents a search for new methods of making ideas and images come alive on the printed page; they have enquiring minds and they are not afraid to make mistakes.

They know their craft and use the technology of the graphic arts creatively, rather than being subdued by it. But above all, they never limit themselves to current tastes, or to formal rules of layout, typography and colour.

London, 1963

Think small.
Our little car isn't so much of a novelty any more.
A couple of dozen college kids don't try to squeeze inside it.
The guy at the gas station doesn't ask where the gas goes.
Nobody even stares at our shape.
In fact, some people who drive our little flivver don't even think 32 miles to the gallon is going any great guns.
Or using five pints of oil instead of five quarts.
Or never needing anti-freeze.
Or racking up 40,000 miles on a set of tires.
That's because once you get used to some of our economies, you don't even think about them any more.
Except when you squeeze into a small parking spot. Or renew your small insurance. Or pay a small repair bill. Or trade in your old VW for a new one.
Think it over.

Graphic design is a means, not an end. The illustration, layout and typography in this advertising campaign do not compete for the readers' attention with the provocative message.

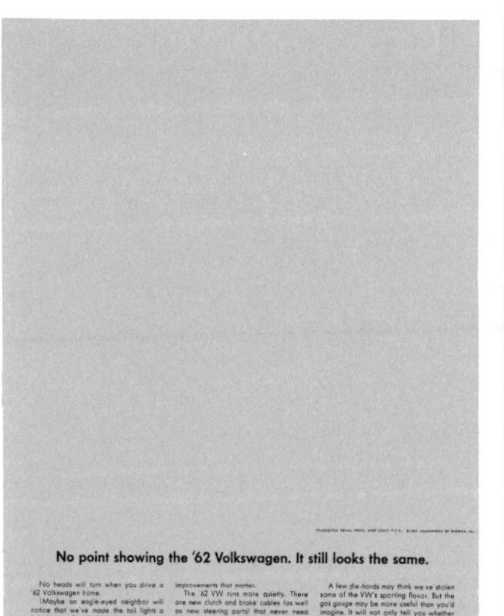
No point showing the '62 Volkswagen. It still looks the same.
No heads will turn when you drive a '62 Volkswagen home.
(Maybe an eagle-eyed neighbor will notice that we've made the tail lights a little bigger. But that's the only clue.)
Everything else on the outside is right where we left it in '61.
Inside is another story.
We've put all our time and effort into improvements that matter.
The '62 VW runs more quietly. There are new clutch and brake cables (as well as new steering parts) that never need maintenance. Heater outlets front and rear for more even heating. Easier braking.
And 24 more.
One change is literally a gasser.
We've added a gas gauge. Our first.
A few die-hards may think we've stolen some of the VW's sporting flavor. But the gas gauge may be more useful than you'd imagine. It will not only tell you whether your tank is E or F; it will prove you're driving a '62.
It could make 1962 go down in VW history as the year of the big change.

The famous Italian designer suggested one change.
Just because the appearance of the Volkswagen doesn't change from year to year, don't think we take it for granted.
Some time ago, we called in a world-famous Italian body designer and we asked him what changes he would recommend in the design of the Volkswagen.
He studied it and studied it. Then he said, "Make the rear window larger."
"That's all?"
"That's all."
We did, starting with the '58 VW.
The Volkswagen is never changed to make it different. Only to make it better.
Changes take place throughout the year. 19 functional improvements have been made in the 1960 VW so far; improvements in handling, in ride, in durability. But your eye wouldn't detect these changes unless we pointed them out. A nice Volkswagen touch is that most of the new parts are interchangeable; they can also be used on previous-year VWs.
We think the Volkswagen approach to automobile design makes sense. It might even turn out to be the most advanced styling idea of all.

A Volkswagen, obviously.
It's easy to spot a Volkswagen.
Even with enough snow on it to hide the beetle shape.
It's the one that keeps moving.
A Volkswagen will even go up icy hills when other cars won't go at all because we put the engine in the back. It gives the rear wheels much better traction.
That's half the problem.
But the engine can't just be there. It has to keep working.
So we cool the VW engine with air, not water. There's no need for anti-freeze, no chance of the block cracking. (No possibility of boiling over in summer, either.) And there's no draining. No flushing. No rust.
You can park a VW outdoors in sub-zero weather or dig it out of a snowbank; it's ready to roll as soon as you turn the key.
If you happen to live where ice and snow are no problem, don't think you can't judge the VW's extraordinary abilities.
Just try it in sand or mud.

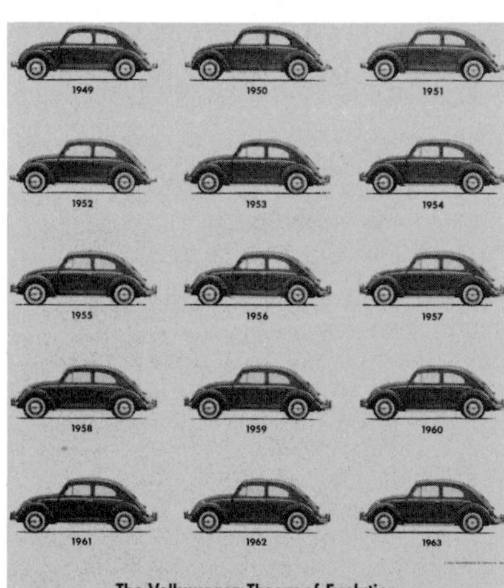
1949
1950
1951
1952
1953
1954
1955
1956
1957
1958
1959
1960
1961
1962
1963
The Volkswagen Theory of Evolution.
Can you spot the Volkswagen with the fins? Or the one that's bigger? Or smaller? Or the one with the fancy chrome work?
You can't?
The reason you can't see any revolutionary design changes on our car is simple: there aren't any.
Now, can you spot the Volkswagen with the synchromesh first gear? Or the one with the more efficient heater? How about the one with the anti-sway bar? Or the more powerful engine?
You can't?
The reason you can't see most of our evolutionary changes is because we've made them deep down inside the car.
And that's our theory: never change the VW for the sake of change, only to make it better.
That's what keeps our car ahead of its time. And never out of style.
Even if you aren't driving the most evolved VW of all.
Our '63.

First you thought small.

And then, of course, someone inevitably comes along and pushes an idea one step further.

Now think a little bigger.

You had the good sense to buy a Volkswagen (or a Renault or a Fiat).

Now you're ready to think a little bigger. And a little faster.

John R. Bond, editor of Road & Track, calls the Peugeot "one of the 7 best made cars in the world." (The other 6: Rolls-Royce, Lancia, Rover, Mercedes-Benz, BMW, Cadillac.) The Rolls costs $15,655, the Rover $3,695, and so forth. The Peugeot 403, however, costs only $2,250* complete. By complete we mean $365 worth of accessories, ranging from reclining seats and sunroof to a silent electric clock.

The Peugeot is a thoughtful car (its 4 doors, for example, open a full 90 degrees; it seats 5 adults in comfort). It is commodious. Quiet. And on the road, it is one of the great driving cars of the generation. You could cruise all day at 80 (if it were legal).

How long will a Peugeot last? The oldest car still running in the United States is an 1891 Peugeot. The "403" is so well made, it costs next to nothing to maintain; last year, warranted Peugeots averaged $6.50 on parts and labor.

If you're looking for a compact car, why not go to your Peugeot dealer (there are 422 of them) and test drive the only compact numbered among the world's 7 best made cars. **PEUGEOT 403**

*P.O.E. EAST AND GULF COAST PORTS/WEST COAST, $2,333.

FOR ILLUSTRATED BROCHURE, WRITE: PEUGEOT, INC., 750 3RD AVE., NEW YORK 17. FOR OVERSEAS DELIVERY, SEE YOUR NEAREST DEALER OR WRITE: CARS OVERSEAS INC., BOX 158, LONG ISLAND CITY 4, N.Y.

ha
ha
(Y)
(Z)

ha
he laughs best (CBS) who laughs last
Some people started laughing right off the bat when they heard we planned to concentrate on comedy this season. They were sure it wouldn't work. These days they're not laughing so hard—but the nation's viewers are, and so are the sponsors of our comedy programs. The audiences attracted by the average comedy program on the three networks this season tell the story: Network Y—7.3 million homes…Network Z—8.9 million homes…CBS Television Network, 9.5 million homes.* Moreover, in the latest Nielsen report three of our funniest shows are in the Top 10—and two of them are brand new this season.† But the thing that keeps all our advertisers smiling is that the CBS Television Network attracts the biggest average audiences in every category of entertainment, laughs or no laughs.
CBS Television Network

It also helps if the designer has a sense of humour.

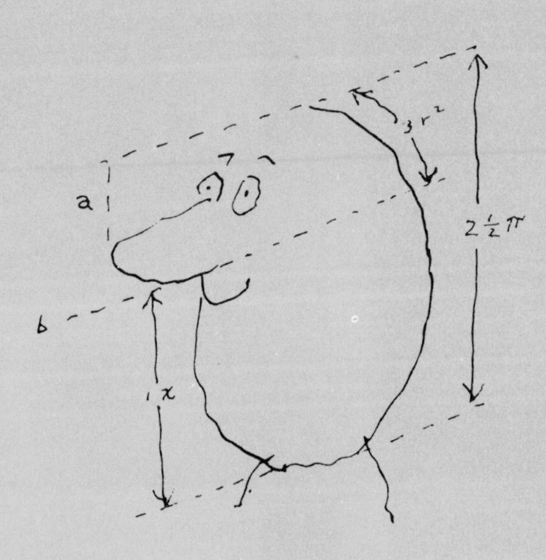

A course in Humorous Illustration will be given by R. O. Blechman at The School of Visual Arts, Wednesday Evenings from 7 to 10, commencing January 30th. Among the topics to be covered in a workshop-lecture series will be Humorous Illustration in Editorial and Advertising Art, Animated Cartoons, Single Panel and Sequence Cartoons. For further information inquire: The School of Visual Arts, 209 East 23rd Street, New York 10, MU 3-8397.

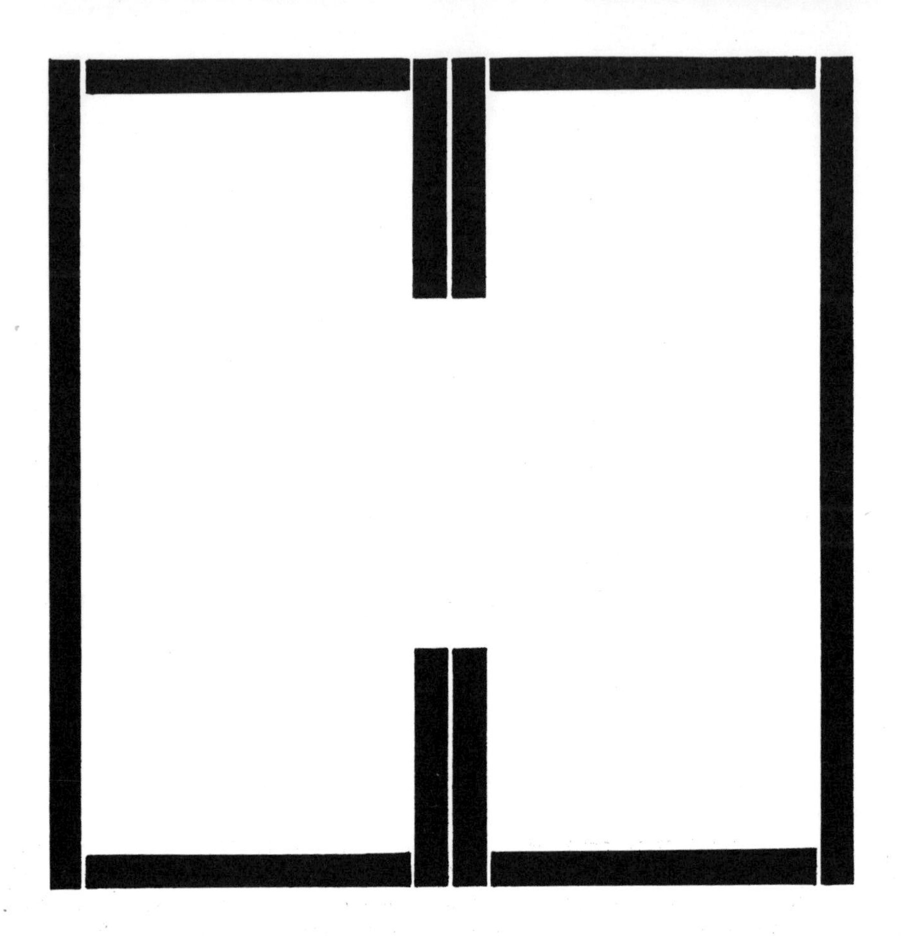

A trademark poses a basic problem. Ideally, it must be simple and distinctive, and must communicate something about the company it represents. This H evolved from the design module of a furniture manufacturer.

his three-dimensional version is architectural; appropriate to a chain of hotels.

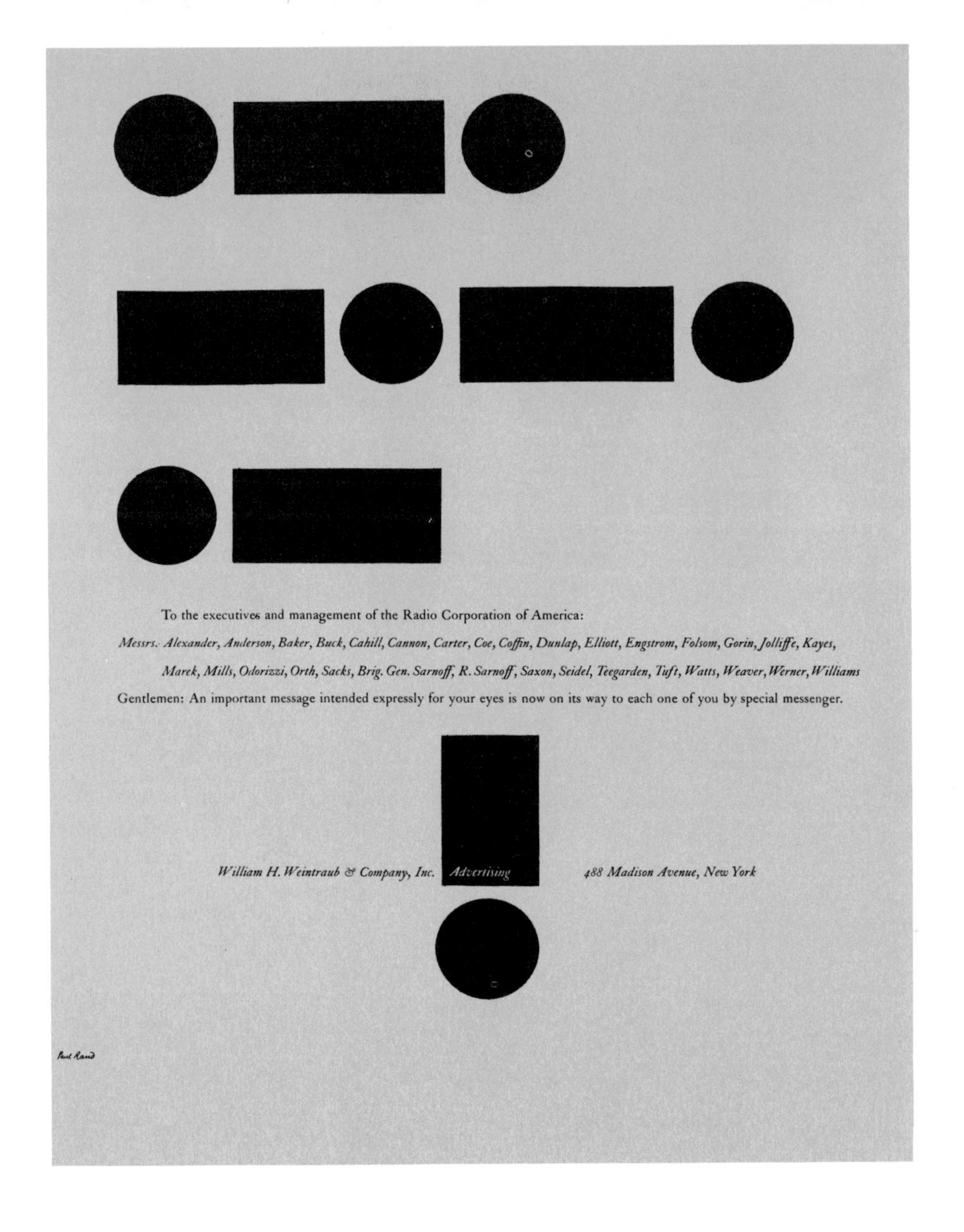
To the executives and management of the Radio Corporation of America:
Messrs. Alexander, Anderson, Baker, Buck, Cahill, Cannon, Carter, Coe, Coffin, Dunlap, Elliott, Engstrom, Folsom, Gorin, Jolliffe, Kayes,
Marek, Mills, Odorizzi, Orth, Sacks, Brig. Gen. Sarnoff, R. Sarnoff, Saxon, Seidel, Teegarden, Tuft, Watts, Weaver, Werner, Williams
Gentlemen: An important message intended expressly for your eyes is now on its way to each one of you by special messenger.
William H. Weintraub & Company, Inc.
Advertising
488 Madison Avenue, New York
Paul Rand

Most symbols have inherent graphic interest. The dots and dashes of the morse code spell R.C.A. Turned on their sides they become an exclamation mark for imphasis, in this advertisement for a radio network.

The seven in this trademark for a film is represented by counting symbols.

SH&L
SH&L Expanded-redesign of
a familiar face. A more flex-
ible version of S&H, long
a favorite of people who
work with fine design.
You can specify SH&L for
a wide range of uses from small
space campaigns to large corporate image projects. We
offer a Bold Face (for impact), Oblique (new ways of view-
ing old problems), and Casual (no straining for mere effect).
For a full showing, call Herb Lubalin at PLaza 1-1250, or
write him c/o SH&L, 130 E. 59th Street, New York 20, N.Y.

Repetition ad infinitum can communicate as well as attract.

A poster for a Book Fair.

The same object can symbolise different things.

HOUSE
265 Old Brompton Rd. SW5

If the designer has a strong personality it will come through whether it is transmitted by his own hand. . .

or by a machine.

A trademark can be manipulated to create many moods and images.

The most effective design is usually utterly simple or exaggerated. A blatantly honest orange used in an advertisement for juice.

An honestly blatant sandwich on a poster for bread.

Sometimes the most effective way to focus on a detail is to show its surroundings.

SHOW
THE MAGAZINE OF THE ARTS
75 CENTS
FEBRUARY 1963
INCORPORATING USA•1
SPACE RACE: TOWARD A RENAISSANCE?
MOTHER TATTLES ON TENNESSEE
"MAY WE BORROW YOUR HUSBAND?" A SHOCKING NEW STORY BY GRAHAM GREENE
OPERA VALENTINE: ANNA MOFFO

prxxxt

private

secredtary

• • • •

CBS televixsiokn

The designer can make capital out of error. A portrait of the haphazard heroine on a television title card.

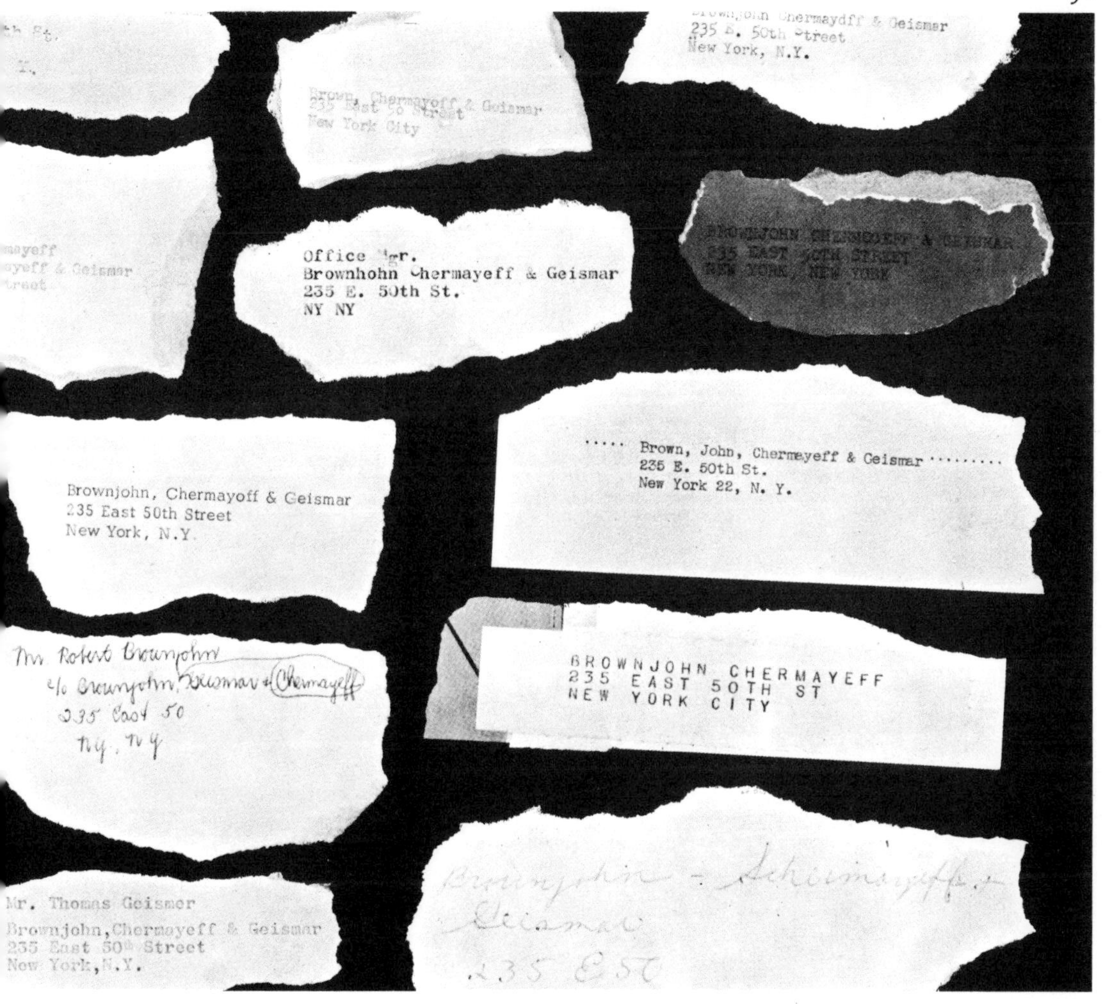

ragments of improperly addressed envelopes used on a poster to draw attention to a name.

Design, in addition to solving specific problems, occasionally, like painting, justifies itself. A variation of a trademark becomes the illustration in this advertisement.

the art of
ASSEM.
BLAGE
the museum of modern art

An exhibition of collage is illustrated on its catalogue cover.

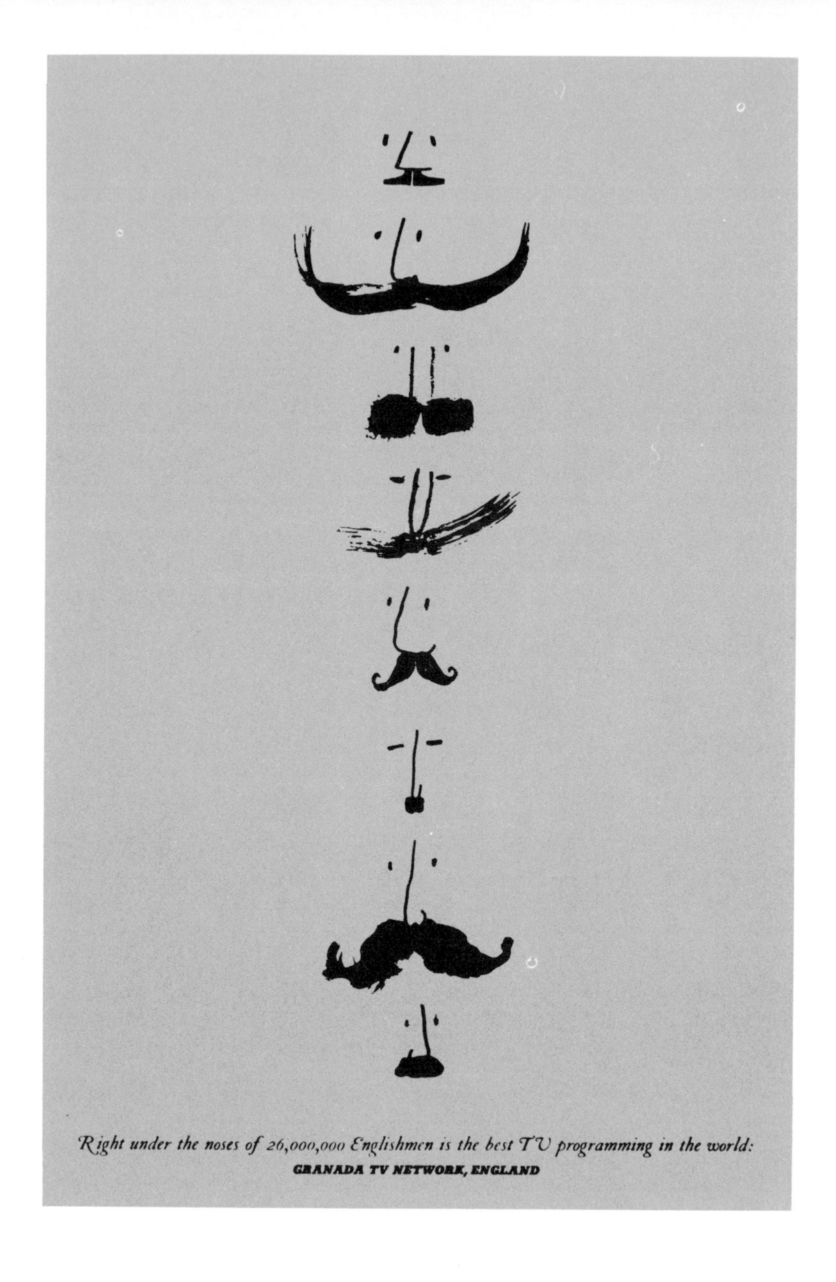
Right under the noses of 26,000,000 Englishmen is the best TV programming in the world:
GRANADA TV NETWORK, ENGLAND

Pictorial detail can re-enforce an idea. An illustration of individuality within a group.

ocial comment on the change of an individual

abcdefghijklmnopqrstuvwxyz

At your public library they've got these arranged in ways that can make you cry, giggle, love, hate, wonder, ponder and understand.

It's astonishing what those twenty-six little marks can do.

In Shakespeare's hands they became *Hamlet*.

Mark Twain wound them into *Huckleberry Finn*. James Joyce twisted them into *Ulysses*. Gibbon pounded them into *The Decline and Fall of the Roman Empire*. Milton shaped them into *Paradise Lost*. Einstein added some numbers and signs (to save time and space) and they formed *The General Theory of Relativity*.

Your name is in them.

And here we are using them now.

Why? Because it's National Library Week—an excellent time to remind you of letters, words, sentences and paragraphs. In short, *books—reading*.

You can live without reading, of course. But it's so *limiting*.

How else can you go to Ancient Rome? Or Gethsemane? Or Gettysburg?

Or meet such people as Aristotle, F. Scott Fitzgerald, St. Paul, Byron, Napoleon, Ghengis Khan, Tolstoi, Thurber, Whitman, Emily Dickinson and Margaret Mead?

To say nothing of Gulliver, Scarlett O'Hara, Jane Eyre, Gatsby, Oliver Twist, Heathcliffe, Captain Ahab, Raskolnikov and Tom Swift?

With books you can climb to the top of Everest, drop to the bottom of the Atlantic. You step upon the Galapagos, sail alone around the world, visit the Amazon, the Antarctic, Tibet, the Nile.

You can learn how to do anything from cooking a carrot to repairing a television set.

With books you can explore the past, guess at the future and make sense out of today.

Read. Your public library has thousands of books, all of which are yours for the asking.

And add books to your *own* library. With each book you add, your home grows bigger and more interesting.

National Library Week, April 16-22

Literal solutions can also be graphic.

a Penguin Book 5/-

Chosen Words

Ivor Brown

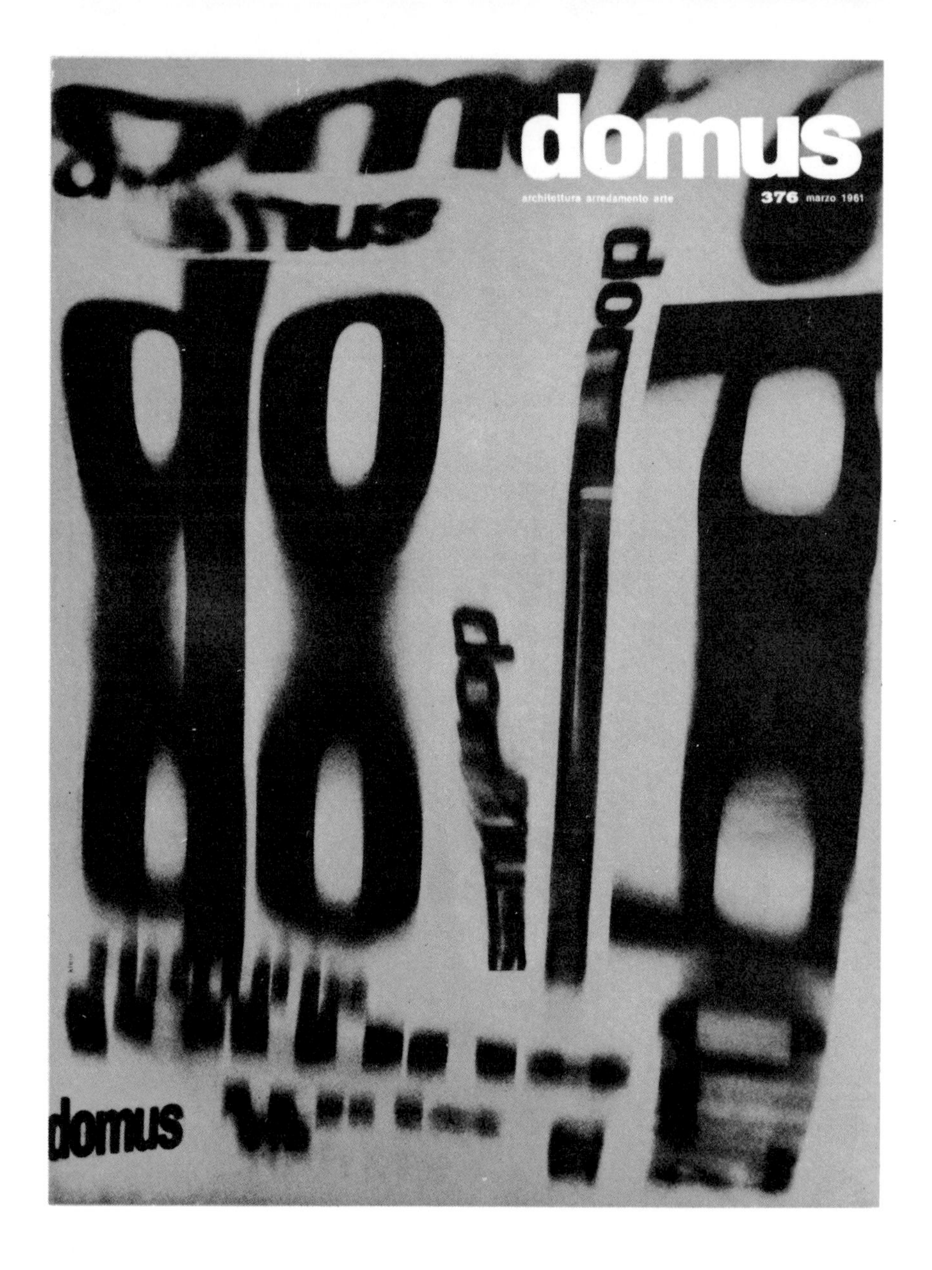

The same design conception can produce different images. Here are two magazine covers solv
the same way but with distinctive results.

92

graphic art; advertising art; applied art
freie graphik; gebrauchsgraphik; angewandte kunst
arts graphiques; arts appliqués; publicité

Alan Fletcher

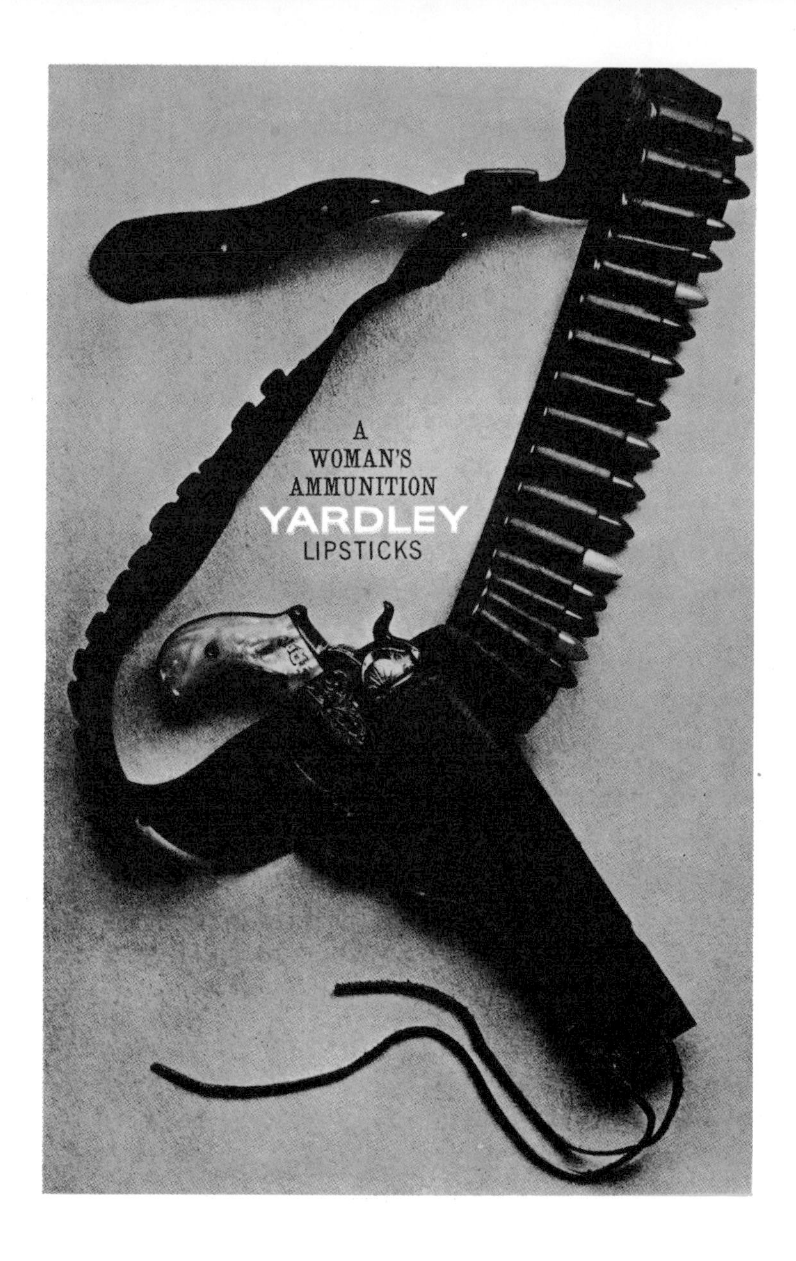

Objects related out of context create new associations. Lipstick becomes feminine ammunition.

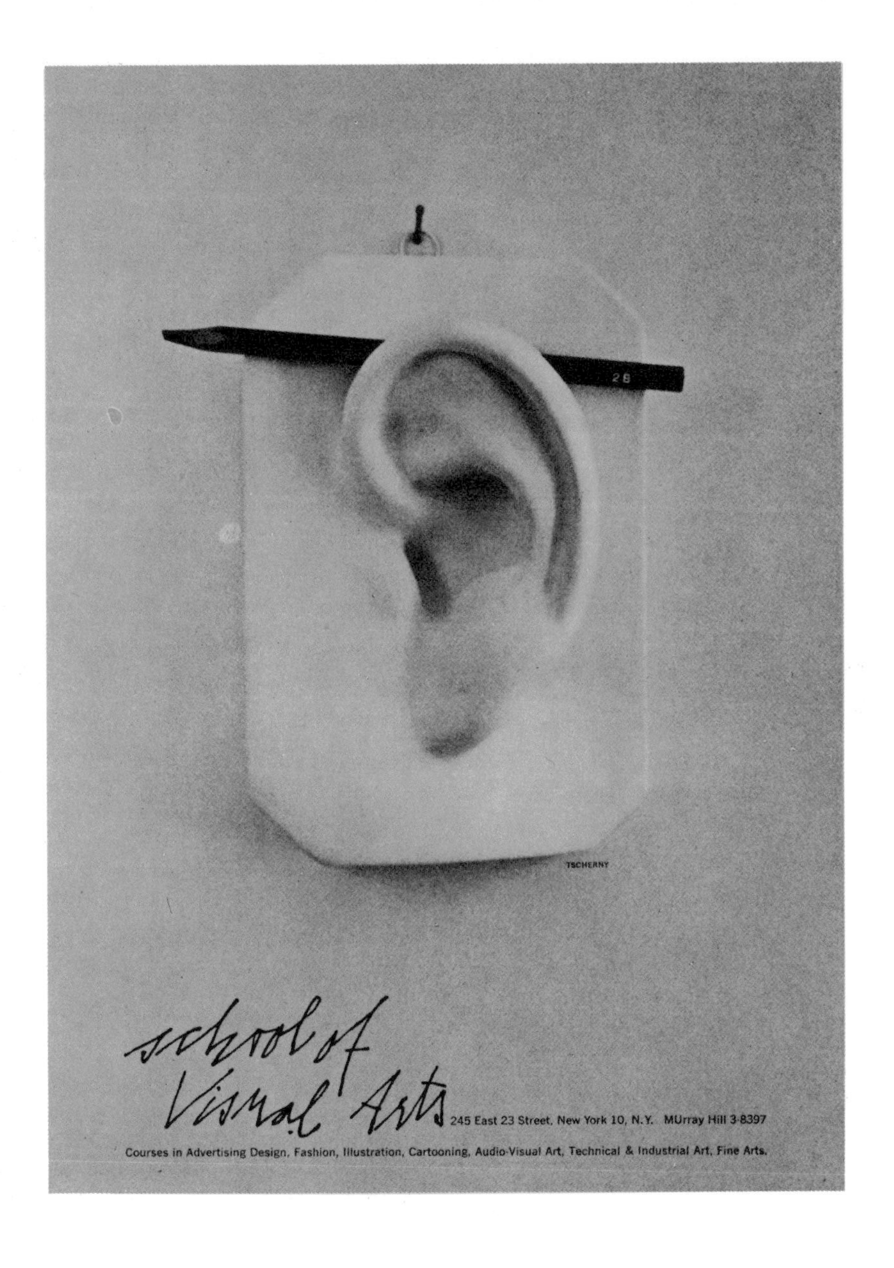

A pencil added to a plaster cast becomes an original symbol for an art school.

ha
lf

addding
subtrcting
multimultiplying
div id ing

aboutface

leaning

st len

o
ver

o

dead

Type can talk. These exerpts from an experimental booklet are a demonstration of words implementing their content.

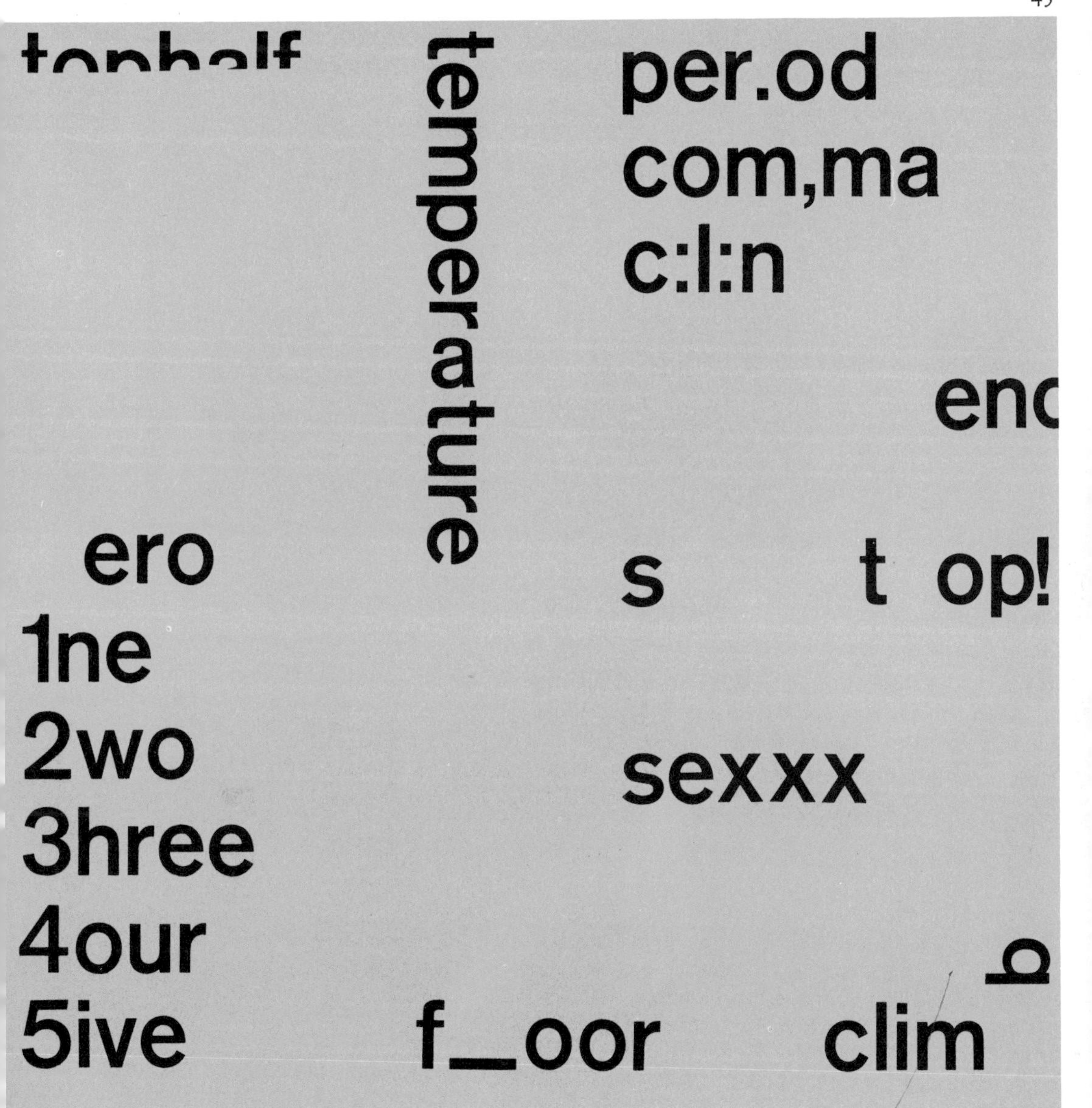
tophalf
temperature
per.od
com,ma
c:l:n
end
ero
s t op!
1ne
2wo
3hree
4our
5ive
sexxx
f_oor
clim b

The basic vocabulary of design can be used to create new forms. An experiment with printing rules.

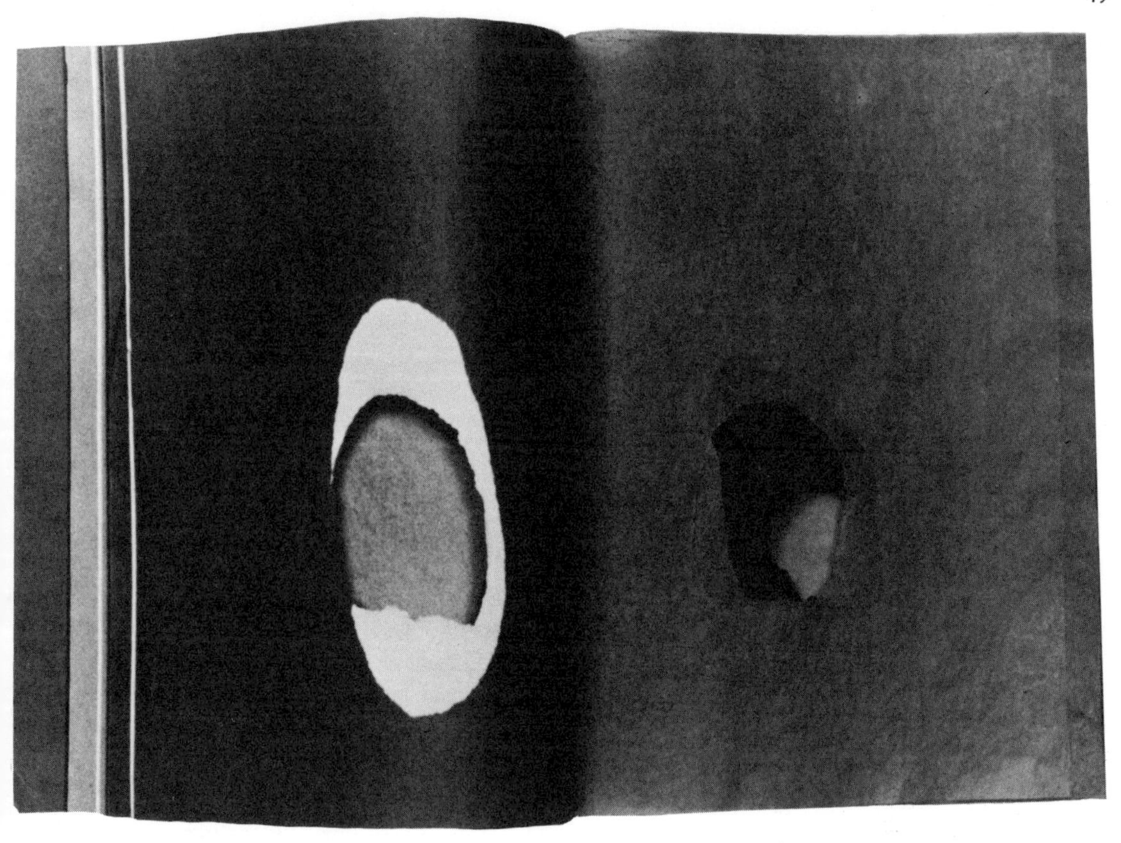

A book without words as a vehicle for collage.

Things which are not essentially visual can be made so.

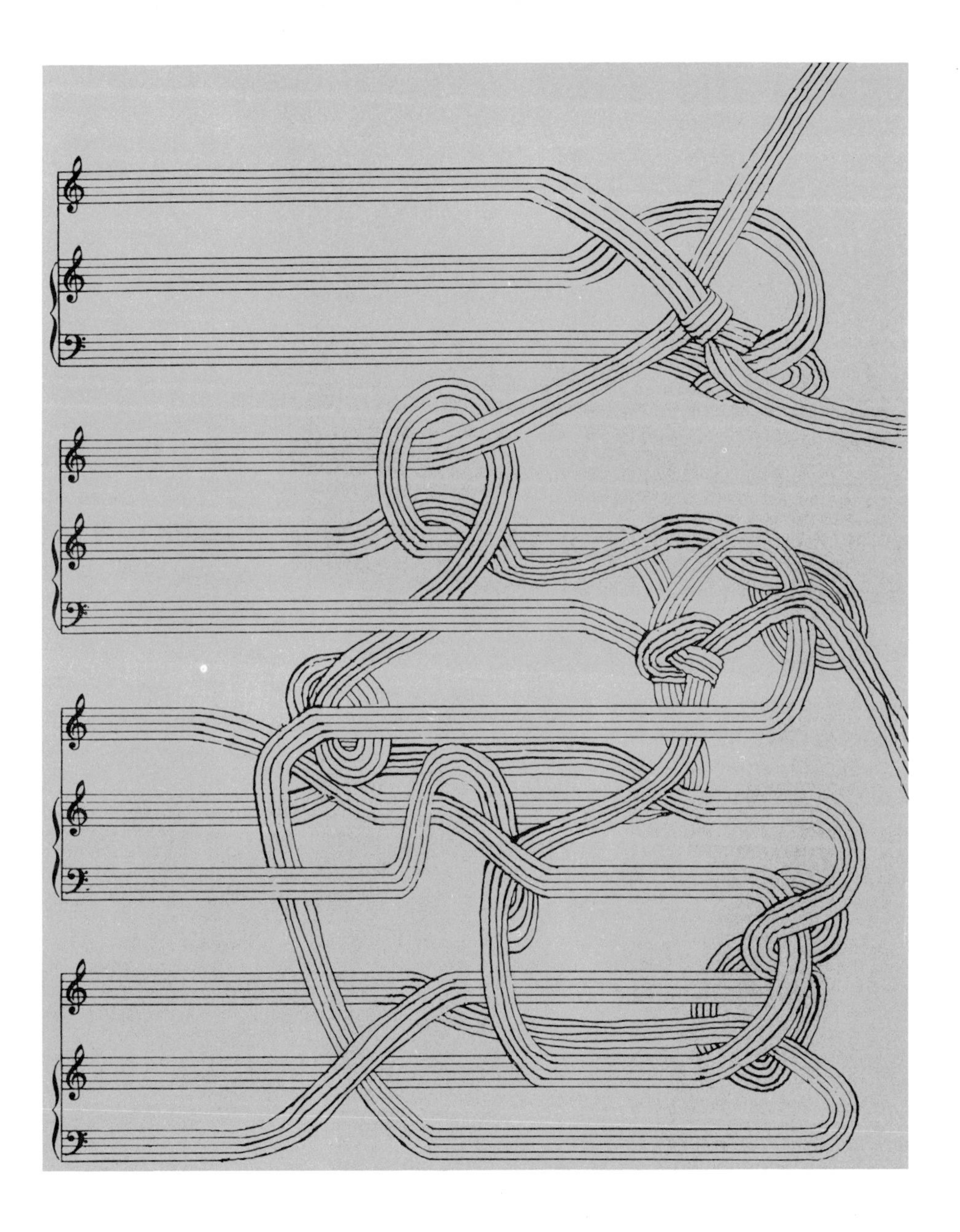

It is possible to *ad lib* graphically. A last minute doodle for a January magazine cover.

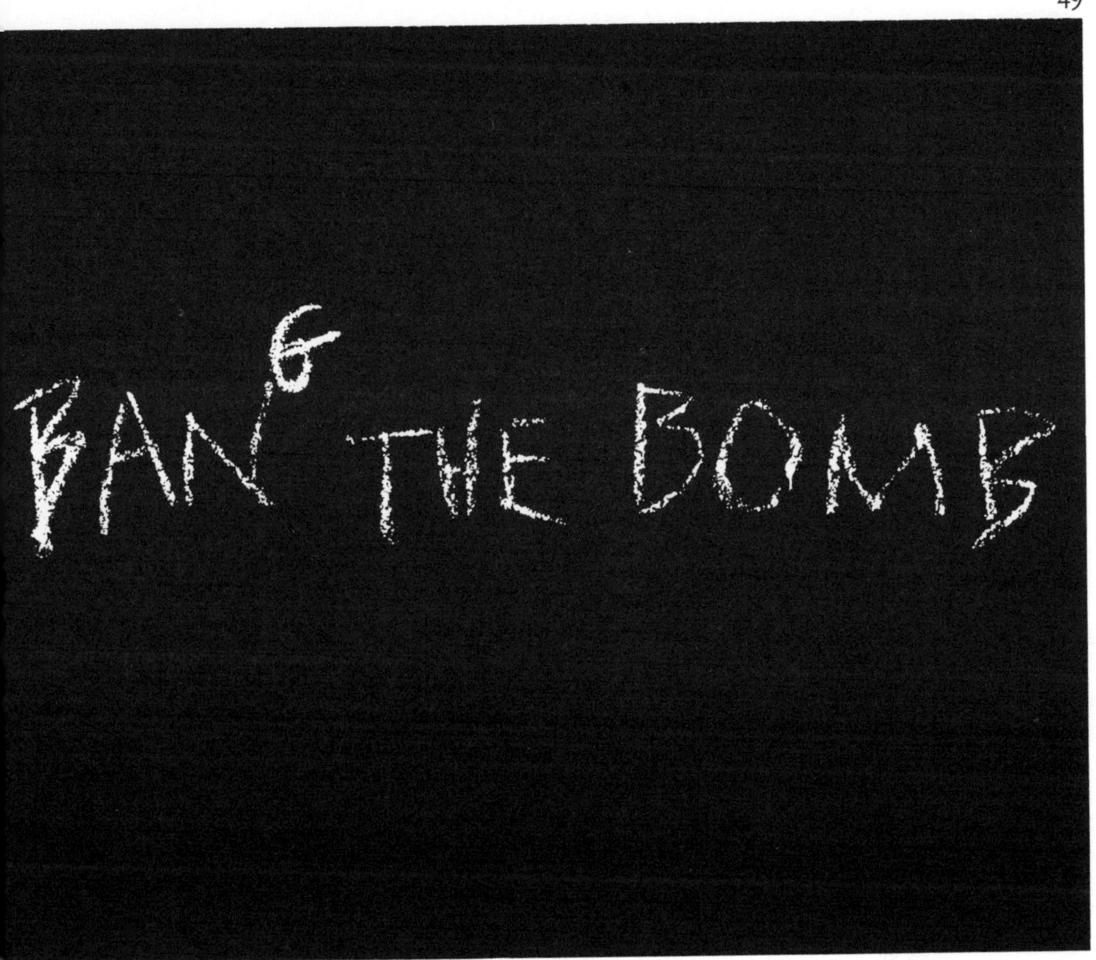

A chalked message for peace on a wall gets transformed.

Graphic objects which are interesting designs in themselves can rarely be altered to advantage. A poster for an exhibition with the Tricolour.

. set of booklets describing an American election.

get the lead out of your ads
A prolific pencil is no substitute for a unique advertising idea.
Creativity is an art not a technique at SH&L. Call PLaza 1-1250.

The middle road of design is usually disastrous. Either go wild as in this advertisement for a design office.

r be precise as in this trademark for a process engraver.

Poetry is as rare in graphics as in literature. An illustration for a children's book.

A magazine cover on the theatre in America.

Typography can create atmosphere. . .

and describe a product, among other things.

Wednesday, April 5, 1961 — VARIETY

Homes—Michigan

Homes—Missouri

Homes—Arkansas

Homes—Louisiana

Homes—Ohio

Homes—Indiana

Homes—Tennessee

Homes—Pennsylvania

Homes—Kentucky

Homes—West Virginia

Homes—Mississippi

Homes—Connecticut

Homes—Virginia

Homes—Alabama

Homes—Vermont

Homes—New York

EXCLUSIVE LISTING!

3/4 MILLION MORE HOMES

A CHOICE INVESTMENT

This season the average nighttime program on the CBS Television Network delivers 785,000 more U.S. homes than the second network, 996,000 more homes than the third. This makes the seventh straight year that our advertisers are winning the biggest nationwide audiences in television. As appraised from A. C. Nielsen Reports 1 October 1960-1 March 1961, 6 to 11 pm, AA basis.

BEST LOCATION

CBS TELEVISION NETWORK

OUTSTANDING VIEW

Homes—Georgia

Homes—New Hampshire

Homes—Massachusetts

Homes—New Jersey

Homes—Maryland

Homes—South Carolina

Homes—Maine

Homes—Rhode Island

Homes—Delaware

Homes—North Carolina

Homes—Florida

Conventional graphics can be used to make unusual backgrounds.

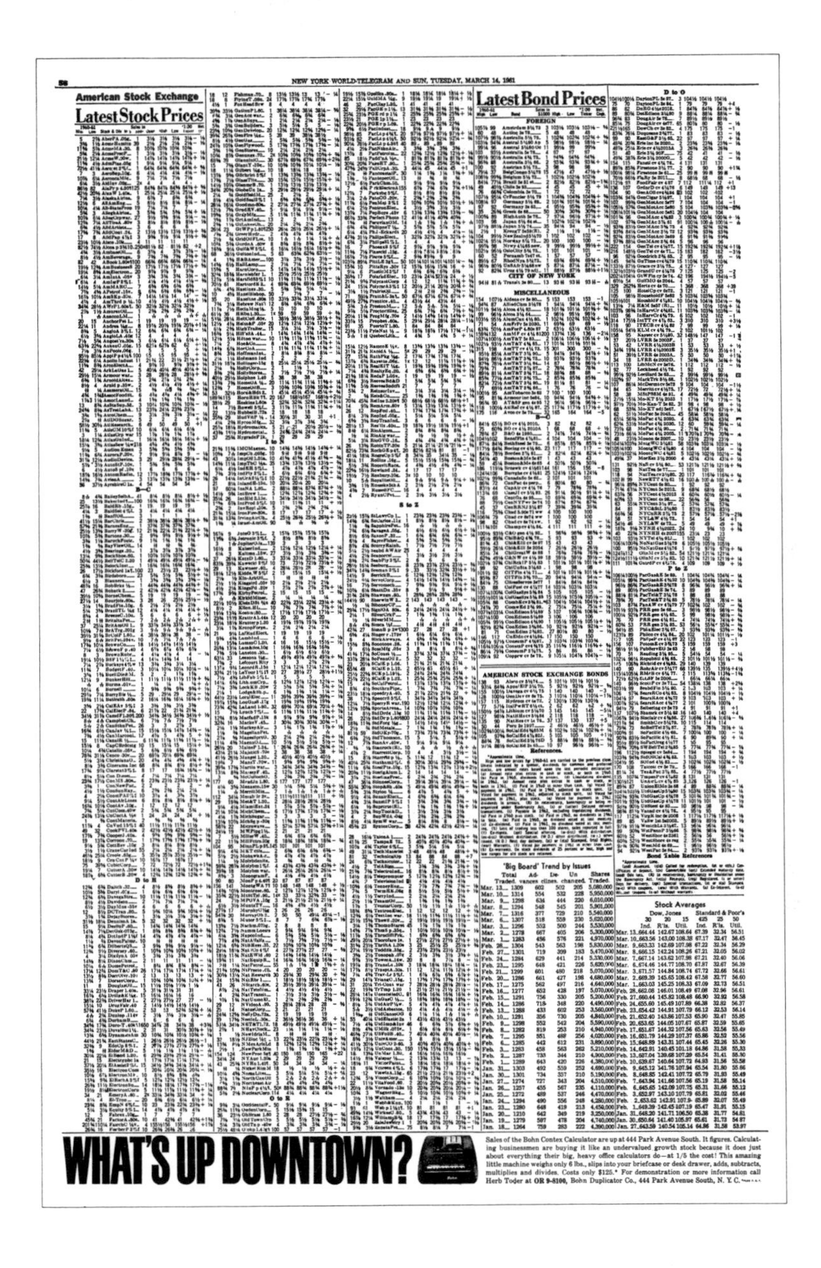

58 NEW YORK WORLD-TELEGRAM AND SUN, TUESDAY, MARCH 14, 1961

American Stock Exchange
Latest Stock Prices

Latest Bond Prices

'Big Board' Trend by Issues

	Total Traded.	Advances	Declines	Unchanged.	Shares Traded.
Mar. 13	1309	602	502	205	5,080,000
Mar. 10	1314	554	532	228	5,950,000
Mar. 9	1298	634	444	220	6,010,000
Mar. 8	1294	548	545	201	5,901,000
Mar. 7	1316	377	729	210	5,540,000
Mar. 6	1307	518	559	230	5,620,000
Mar. 3	1296	552	500	244	5,530,000
Mar. 2	1278	667	405	206	5,300,000
Mar. 1	1283	486	576	221	4,970,000
Feb. 28	1304	543	563	198	5,830,000
Feb. 27	1301	719	399	183	5,470,000
Feb. 24	1284	629	441	214	5,330,000
Feb. 23	1295	648	421	226	5,620,000
Feb. 21	1299	601	480	218	5,070,000
Feb. 20	1286	661	427	198	4,680,000
Feb. 17	1275	562	497	216	4,640,000
Feb. 16	1277	652	428	197	5,070,000
Feb. 15	1291	756	330	205	5,200,000
Feb. 14	1286	718	348	220	4,490,000
Feb. 13	1288	433	602	253	3,560,000
Feb. 10	1291	356	730	205	4,840,000
Feb. 9	1298	552	542	204	5,590,000
Feb. 8	1282	819	253	210	4,940,000
Feb. 7	1295	551	488	256	4,020,000
Feb. 6	1285	442	612	231	3,890,000
Feb. 3	1283	458	563	262	5,210,000
Feb. 2	1287	733	344	210	4,900,000
Feb. 1	1289	643	420	226	4,380,000
Jan. 31	1303	492	559	252	4,690,000
Jan. 30	1301	734	357	210	5,190,000
Jan. 27	1274	727	343	204	4,510,000
Jan. 26	1257	455	567	235	4,110,000
Jan. 25	1272	489	537	246	4,470,000
Jan. 24	1294	490	556	248	4,280,000
Jan. 23	1280	648	419	213	4,450,000
Jan. 20	1210	642	349	219	3,250,000
Jan. 19	1279	597	478	204	4,740,000
Jan. 18	1264	759	283	222	4,390,000

Stock Averages

	Dow, Jones 30 Ind.	Dow, Jones 20 R'ls.	Dow, Jones 15 Util.	Standard & Poor's 425 Ind.	Standard & Poor's 25 R'ls.	Standard & Poor's 50 Util.
Mar. 13	664.44	142.67	108.64	67.39	32.34	56.51
Mar. 10	663.56	143.00	108.38	67.17	32.47	56.45
Mar. 9	663.33	142.69	107.98	67.22	32.34	56.29
Mar. 8	666.15	142.24	108.26	67.21	32.05	56.02
Mar. 7	667.14	143.62	107.98	67.21	32.40	56.06
Mar. 6	674.46	144.77	108.70	67.87	32.67	56.39
Mar. 3	671.57	144.84	108.74	67.72	32.66	56.61
Mar. 2	669.39	145.65	108.42	67.58	32.77	56.60
Mar. 1	663.03	145.25	108.33	67.09	32.73	56.51
Feb. 28	662.08	146.01	108.49	67.08	32.96	56.61
Feb. 27	660.44	145.82	108.48	66.90	32.92	56.58
Feb. 24	655.60	145.49	107.89	66.38	32.82	56.37
Feb. 23	654.42	144.91	107.79	66.12	32.53	56.14
Feb. 21	652.40	143.86	107.53	65.90	32.47	55.85
Feb. 20	653.65	144.05	107.67	65.87	32.59	55.65
Feb. 17	651.67	144.32	107.56	65.63	32.56	55.49
Feb. 16	651.79	144.29	107.37	65.86	32.52	55.56
Feb. 15	648.89	143.31	107.44	65.45	32.26	55.30
Feb. 14	642.91	140.45	101.18	64.86	31.58	55.33
Feb. 13	637.04	139.68	107.29	65.54	31.41	55.30
Feb. 10	639.67	140.64	107.72	64.93	31.56	55.58
Feb. 9	645.12	141.76	107.94	65.54	31.80	55.66
Feb. 8	648.85	142.41	107.72	65.79	31.93	55.49
Feb. 7	643.94	141.66	107.56	65.19	31.58	55.14
Feb. 6	645.65	142.09	107.75	65.31	31.66	55.12
Feb. 3	652.97	143.10	107.79	65.81	32.02	55.46
Feb. 2	653.62	142.91	107.9-	65.89	32.07	55.49
Feb. 1	649.39	142.45	107.19	65.47	31.91	55.15
Jan. 31	648.20	141.71	106.50	65.38	31.77	54.81
Jan. 30	650.64	141.40	105.97	65.61	31.73	54.87
Jan. 27	643.59	140.54	105.14	64.86	31.58	53.97

Another full page advertisement made to appear as if the advertiser could afford only a small space.

Graphic solutions should use the environment to advantage. A bus on a poster.

A poster on a bus.

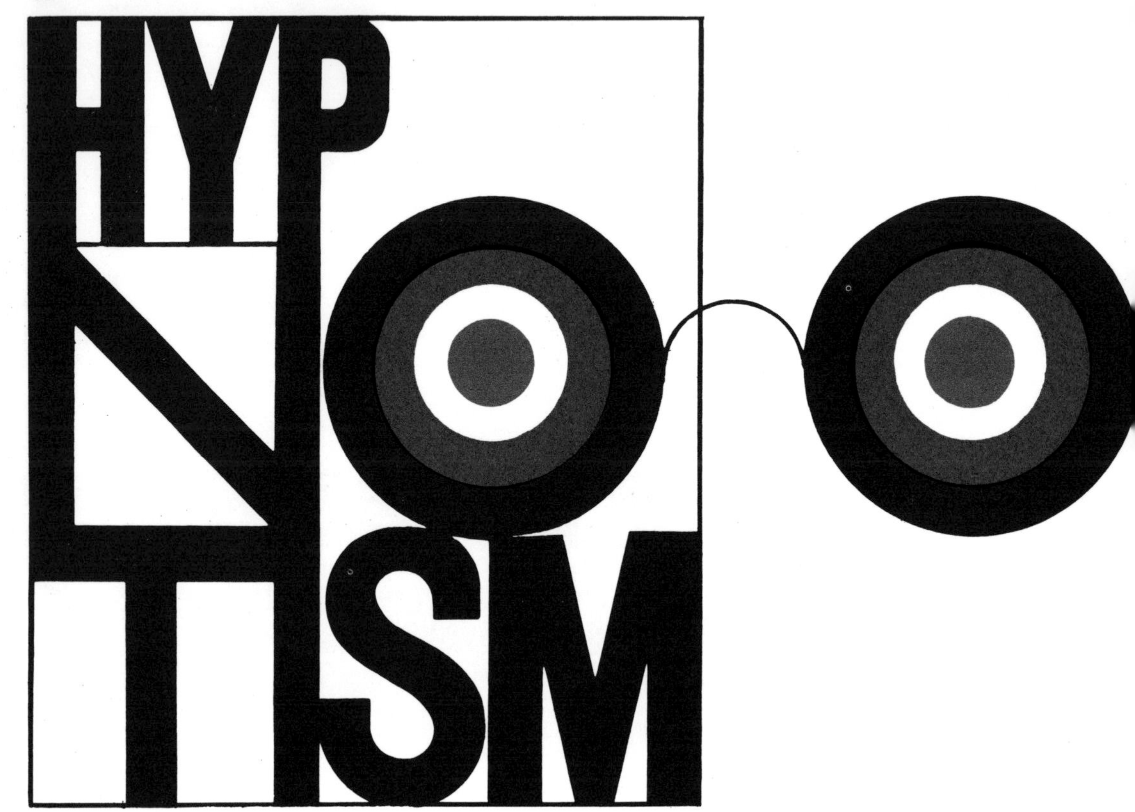

Objects become stylised through simplification. A bizarre image on a book jacket.

trademark for a television network.

Athens is just a stone's throw away.
Greece must have something. Lots of people seem to be going there. Maybe because there's a little Greek in us all.
(This paragraph was a Greek invention. Your doctor took a Greek oath. Democracy was a Greek idea.)
Airplanes, of course, had to wait for the Wright Brothers. But it was worth it. Now you can fly EL AL direct to Athens from New York without even changing planes.
If you already happen to be in Europe with a Grecian yearn, we can zip you to Athens quicker than you can say Parthenon.
And once you're in Athens, you might like to visit our own home town, Tel Aviv. It's only an hour and forty minutes away.
(If you buy a round trip ticket to Tel Aviv in the first place, you can stop at Athens and 28 other cities at no extra charge.)
So if you'd like to tread where Aristotle trod, call your travel agent or EL AL Israel Airlines, PL 1-7500.
EL AL

The images of contemporary design come from all periods of art and decoration.

Iore classical cribbing.

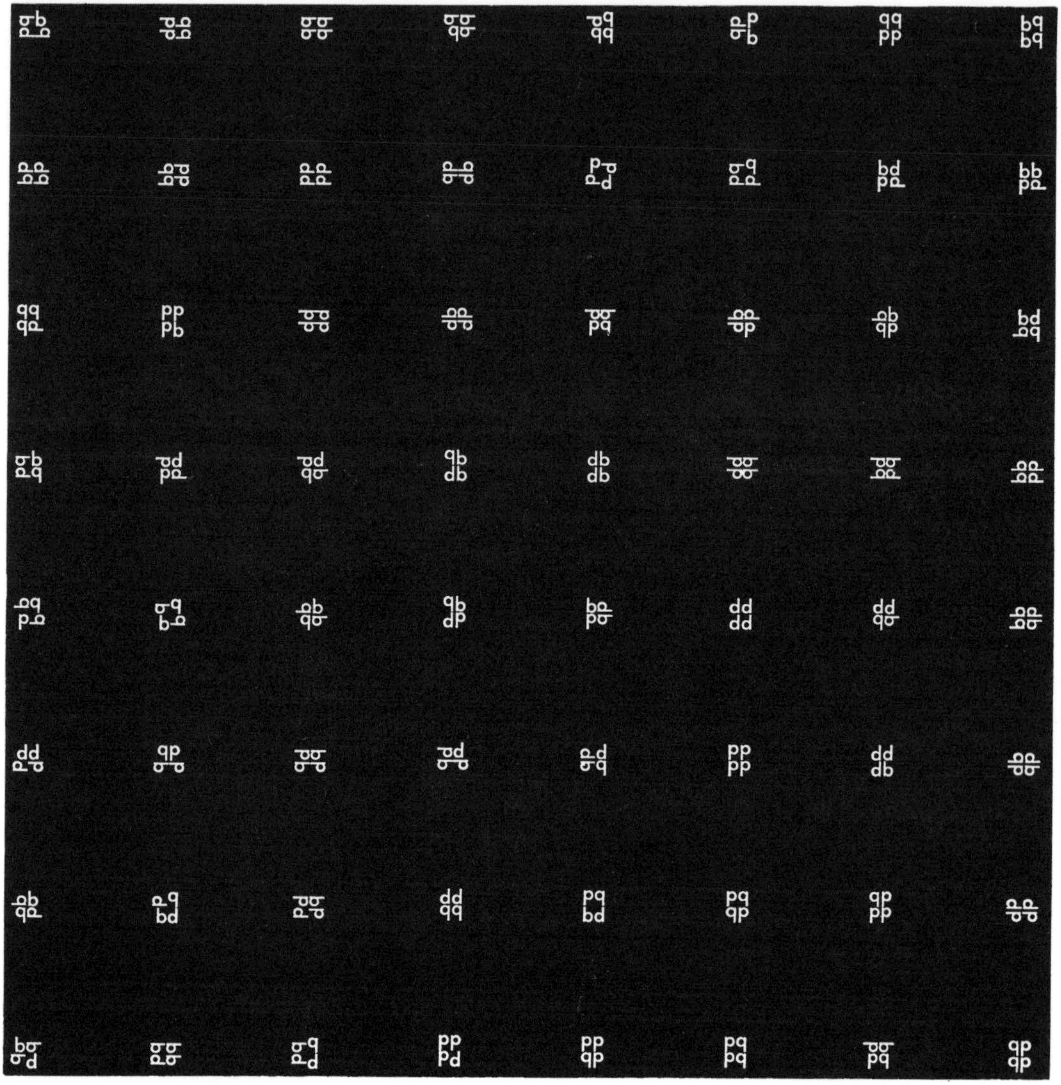

Variety can be achieved with very limited means. A typographic exercise.

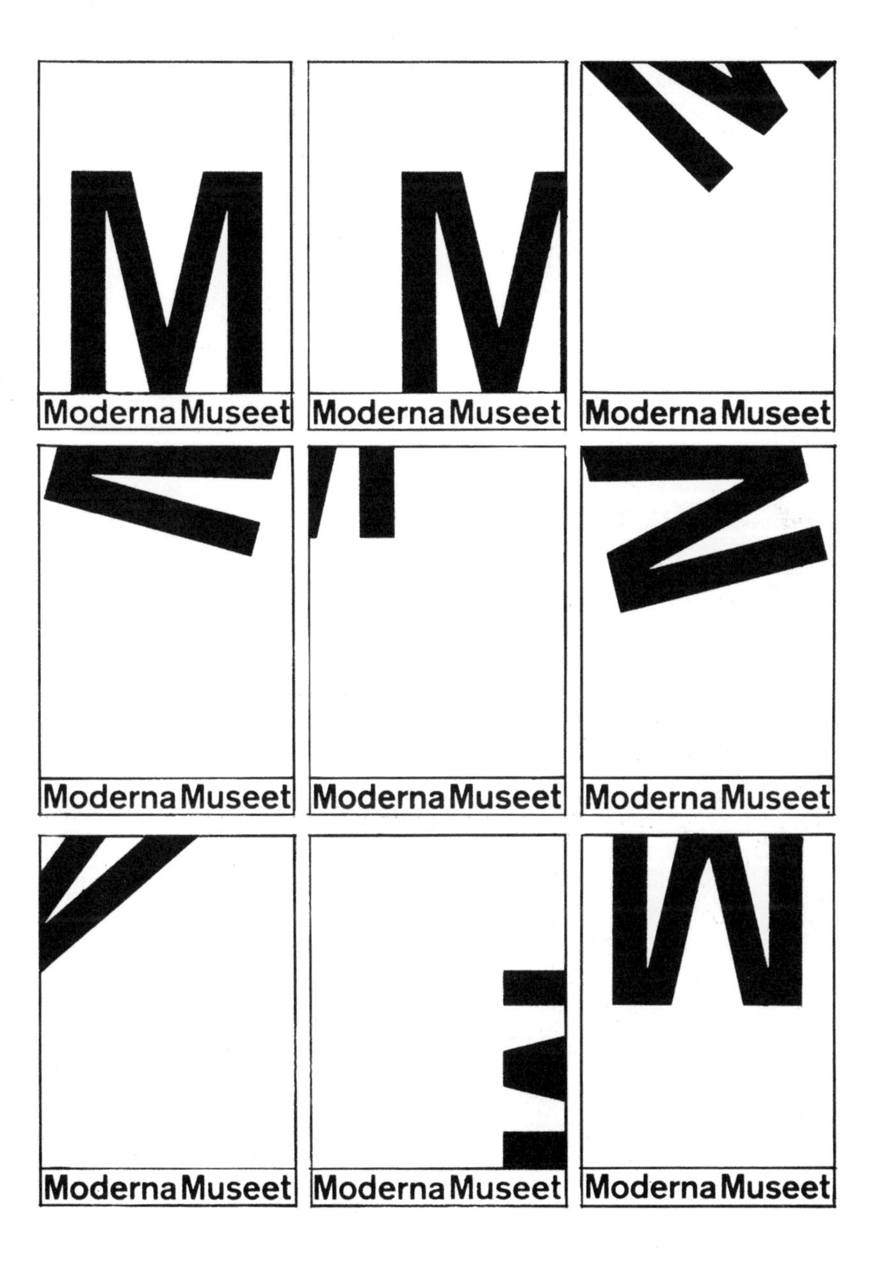

series of posters for a museum.

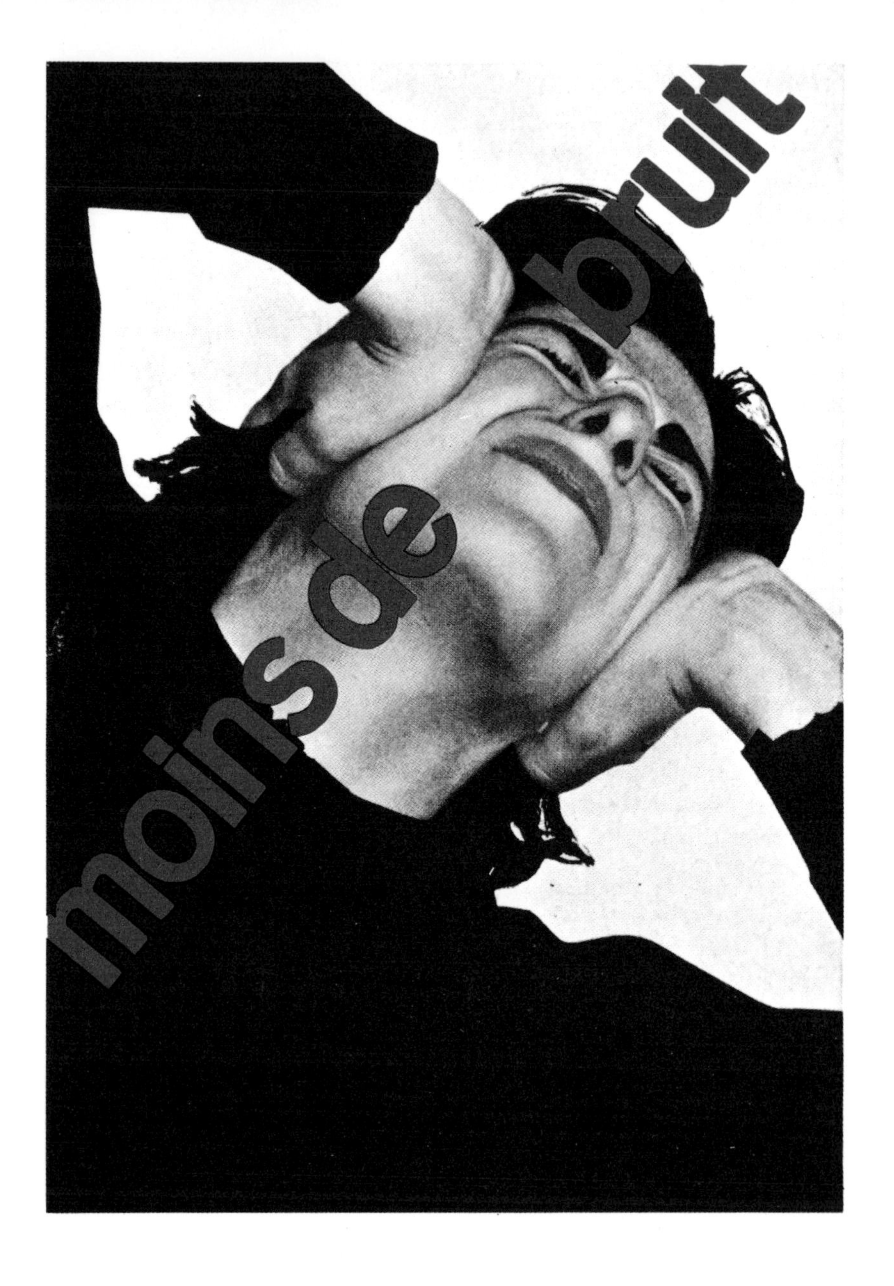

Graphics, in addition to communicating, should be able to evoke an emotional response. A loud anti-noise poster.

trademark for a sentimental film.

The
HEEL,
said Chris-
topher Marlowe,
was invented by a
woman who was al-
ways being kissed on
the forehead. Undeniably,
it raises her stature, giv-
ing her footing and ele-
vation. This is done not
by inches alone, but
with a sizable meas-
ure of savoir faire.
A **DELMAN** heel is
a trompe-l'oeil par
excellence. It abbreviates the foot,
lengthens the body, lightens the car-
riage, takes inches off the hips, and gives
the costume altogether new dimension. She
who walks in beauty, walks in **DELMAN** heel

An ideogram is a fusion of type into form. It can produce an elegant shoe. . .

nd electronic waves

A primitive solution is refreshing when competition is sophisticated. A magazine trademark i
cut in six ways to represent various budgets.

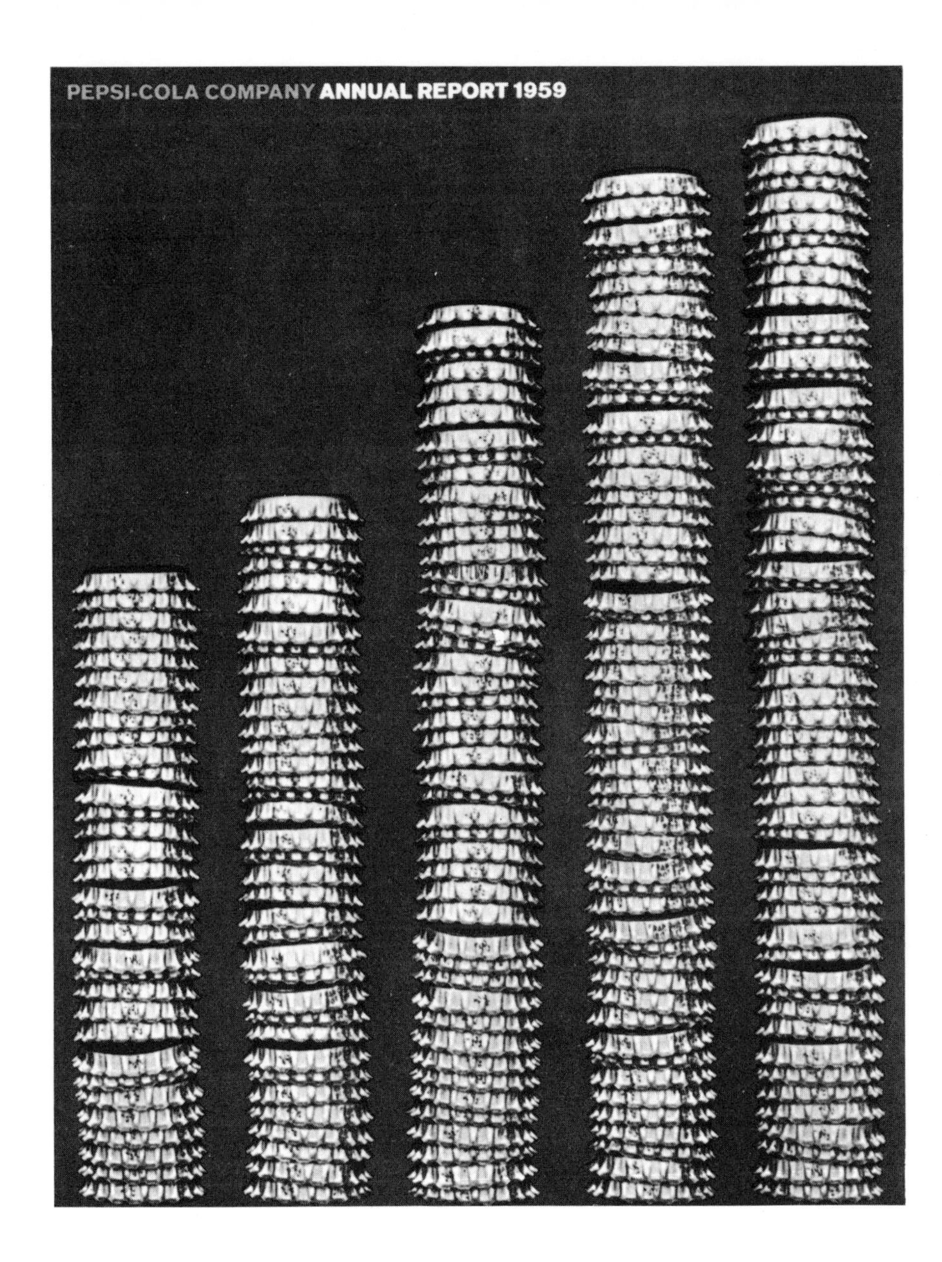

Bottle-tops make a graph on a cover of a soft drink annual report.

Ever since a

ROCK

was a stone

and a

was a bun . . .

Substitution or addition makes letters superfluous . . .

She's got to
go out
to get Woman's Day
the A&P magazine

or indispensable.

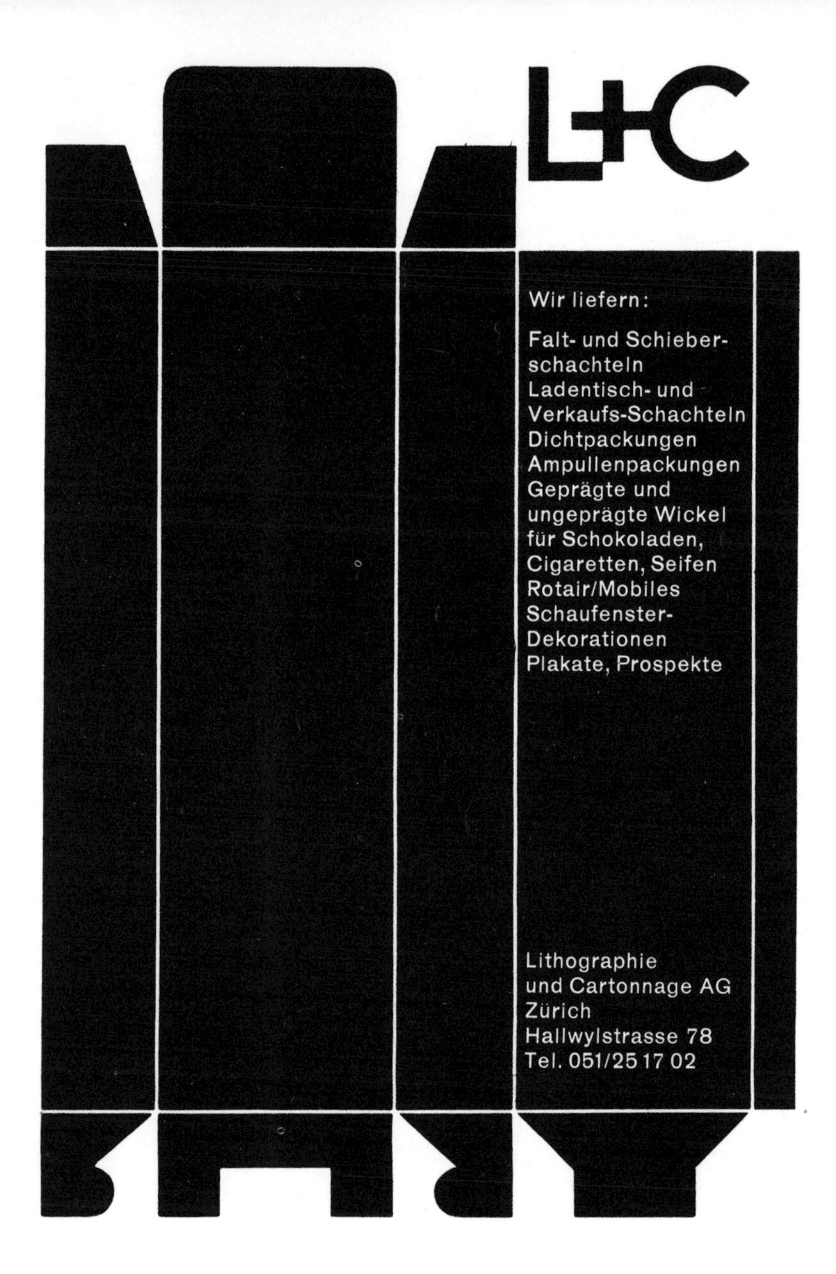
L+C
Wir liefern:
Falt- und Schieber-
schachteln
Ladentisch- und
Verkaufs-Schachteln
Dichtpackungen
Ampullenpackungen
Geprägte und
ungeprägte Wickel
für Schokoladen,
Cigaretten, Seifen
Rotair/Mobiles
Schaufenster-
Dekorationen
Plakate, Prospekte
Lithographie
und Cartonnage AG
Zürich
Hallwylstrasse 78
Tel. 051/25 17 02

The character of a product suggests its rigid.

or fluid rendering.

Each problem has many solutions. Here are two interpretations of 'The Americanisation of Paris'. A magazine cover.

An editorial illustration.

Negative as well as positive space can be dynamic. A page from an experimental booklet on typography.

A trademark for a steel company.

Unusual production techniques can be used to support a statement. An unusual fold creates distortion in this booklet on television comedy.

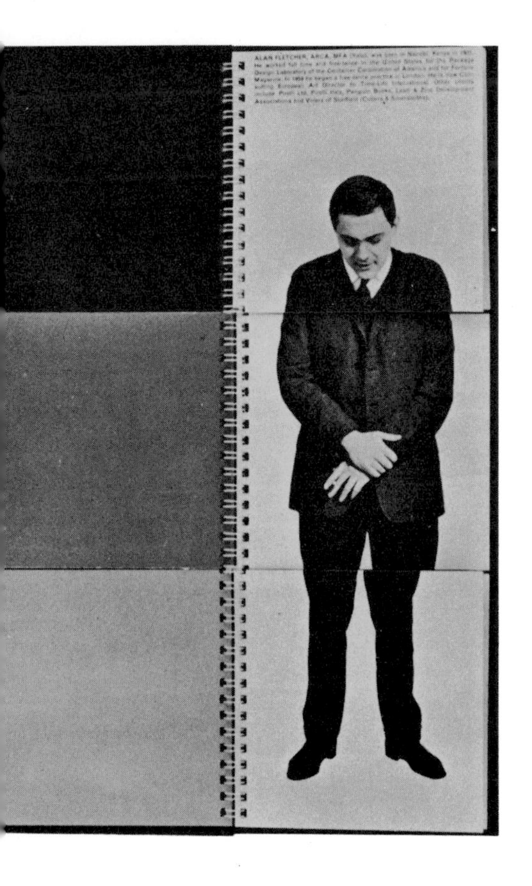

n this announcement of the merger of three designers the binding is split so that their hotographs can interplay.

Comic book clichés can also inspire original graphics.

1.
2.
3.
HAËK

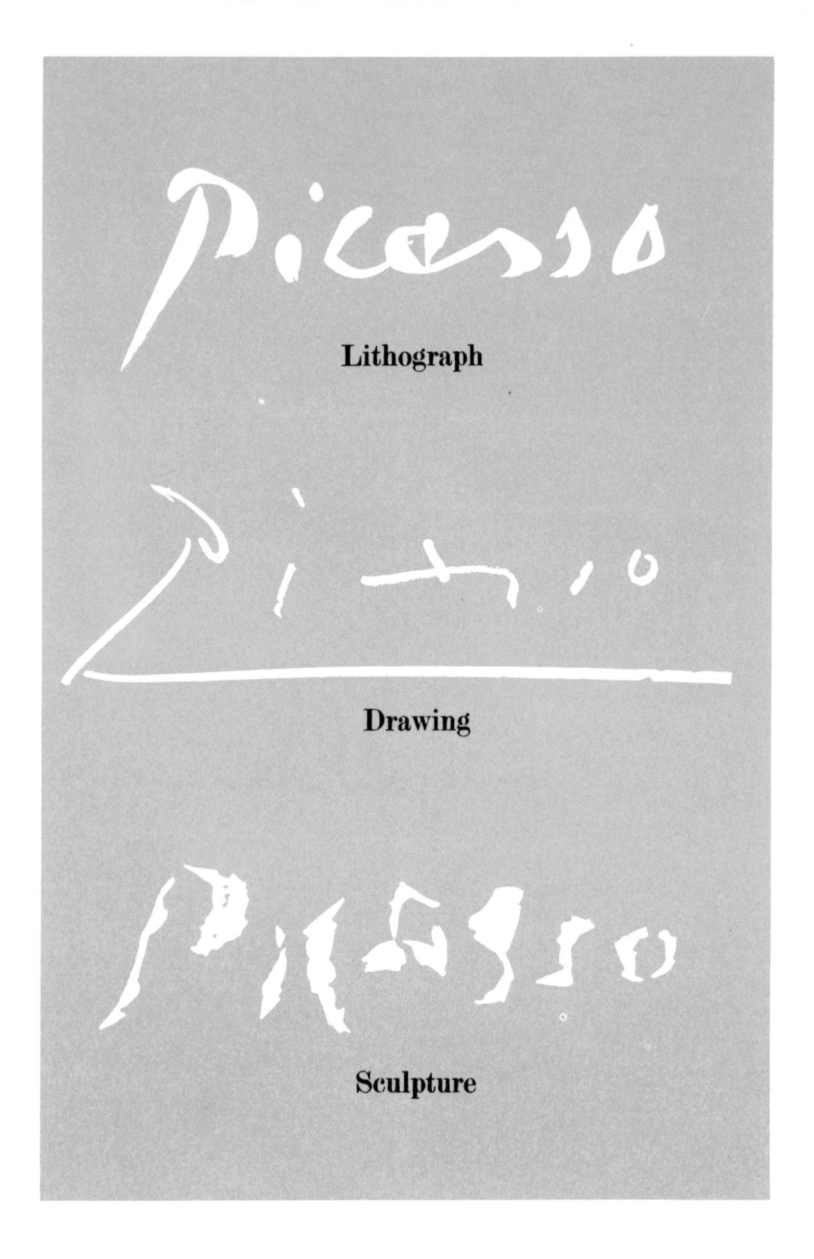

Designers should be capable of magnifying differences to make a point. Three signatures of an artist represent three aspects of his work.

One word by three designers for their Christmas card.

m
h
i
g
two big dates
on your promotion
calendar

Often the parts are more interesting than the whole. The tailors' patterns represent the clothing industry on this booklet cover.

'he plastic components of the rose bring out the fact that it is artificial.

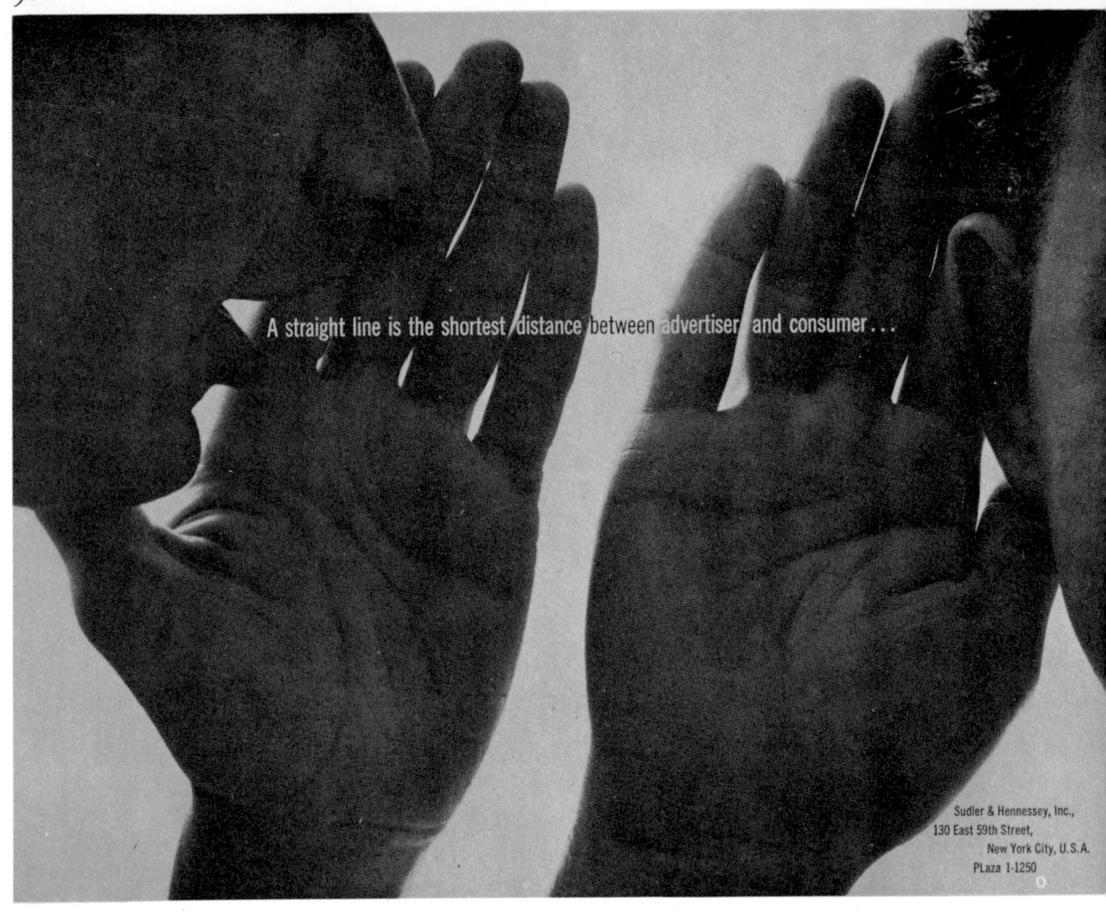
A straight line is the shortest distance between advertiser and consumer...
Sudler & Hennessey, Inc.,
130 East 59th Street,
New York City, U.S.A.
PLaza 1-1250

More non-visual material made visual with imagination. . .

"John, is that Billy coughing?"
"Get up and give him some Coldene."

and some typography.

New trademarks can evolve from standard symbols. Here are two for electrical companies.

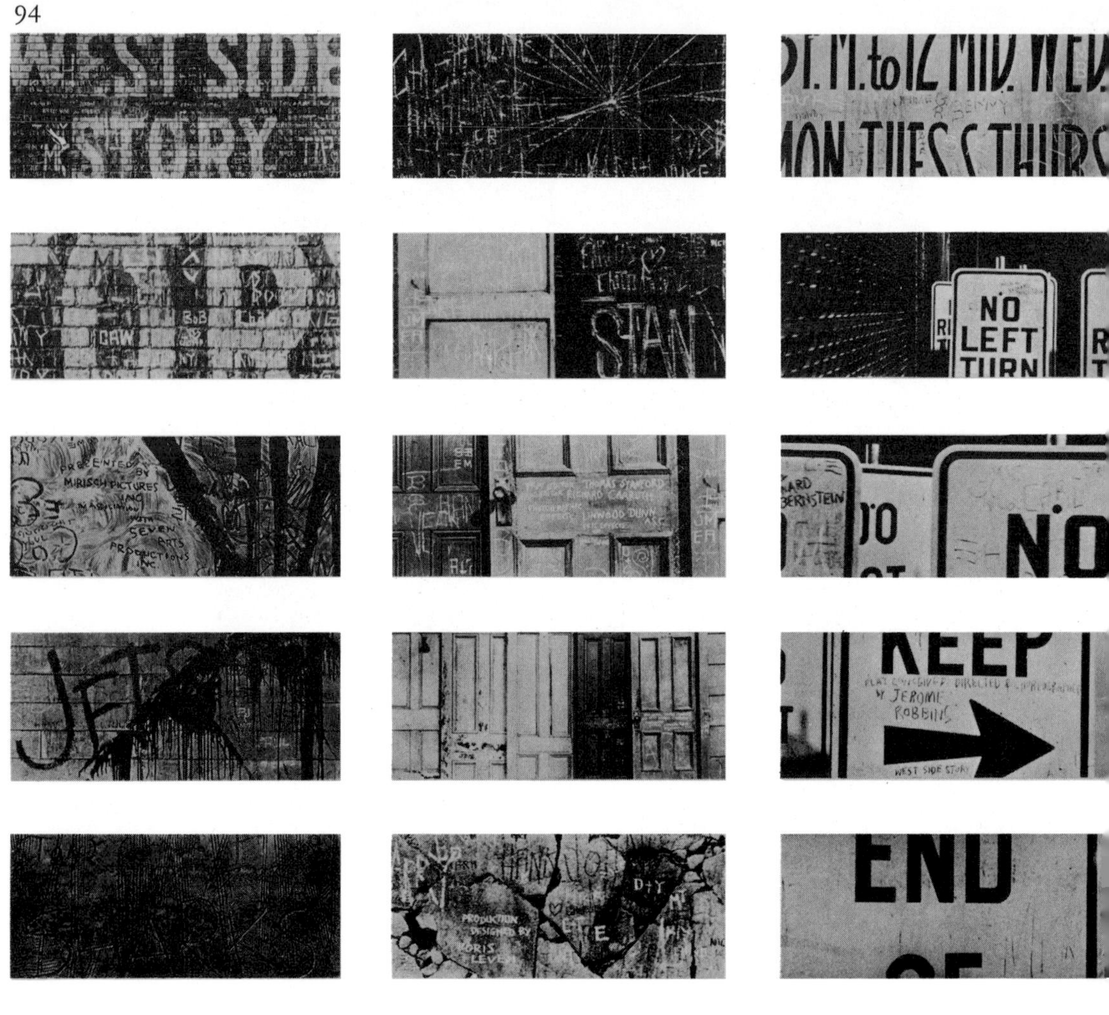

Grafiti and street signs furnish ready-made graphic material. Most designers seem too eager invent shapes and colours that are far less interesting than those provided by reality. The end title for a film about New York City slum-life.

edits

)
agazine advertising
mpaign
olkswagen
obert Levenson,
lien Koenig,
elmut Krone,
ingate Paine,
avid Reider, USA

-11
agazine advertisement
ugeot
eorge Lois, USA

ewspaper advertisement
B.S. Television
etwork
uis Dorfsman,
Amato, USA

nouncement Card
hool of Visual Arts
O. Blechman, USA

ademark
oltzapfel furniture
erstner+Kutter,
vitzerland

ademark
otel Corporation
orman Ives, USA

ewspaper
lvertisement
dio Corporation
America
ul Rand, USA

lm trademark
agnificent Seven
ul Bass, USA

agazine Advertisement
dler,
ennessy & Lubalin
erb Lubalin,
ave Herzbrun, USA

19
Poster
Holland Book Fair
Total Design, Holland

20
Poster
Tribune De Lausanne
Herbert Leupin,
Switzerland

21
Poster
Troubadour Coffee House
Fletcher/Forbes/Gill, UK

22
Designers Signature
Hans Schleger, UK

23
Trademark
Irwin Studio Limited
Robert Brownjohn, UK

24
Magazine Advertisement
Pirelli, spA
André François, France

25
Magazine Advertisement
Pirelli, spA
Bob Noorda, Italy

26
Newspaper
Advertisement
Eversweet Corporation.
Paula Green,
Sidney Meyers, USA

27
Poster
Levy's Bread
William Taubin, USA

28
Poster
Bal du Cinema
R. Savignac, France

29
Magazine Cover
Show
Henry Wolf, USA

30
Television Title
C.B.S. Television
Network
Bob Gill, USA

31
Poster
Brownjohn,
Chermayeff & Geismar,
USA

32
Magazine Advertisement
Olivetti
Giovanni Pintori, Italy

33
Catalogue Cover
Museum of Modern Art
Chermayeff & Geismar
Associates, USA

34
Newspaper
Advertisement
Granada Television
George Loiş,
Tony Palladino, USA

35
Cartoon
Swiat Magazine
Jan Lenica, Poland

36
Newspaper
Advertisement
National Library Week
Monte Ghertler,
Charles Piccirillo, USA

37
Book Jacket
Penguin Books
Derek Birdsall, UK

38
Magazine Cover
Domus
William Klein, France

39
Magazine Cover
Graphis
Alan Fletcher, UK

40
Magazine Advertisement
Yardley Lipstick
Angela Landels, UK

41
Magazine Advertisement
School of Visual Arts
George Tscherny, USA

42-43
Booklet
'Watching Words Move'
Brownjohn, Chermayeff
& Geismar, USA

44
Illustration
'Book 4a, 1961'
Diter Rot, Iceland

45
Double Spread
'Libri Illegibile'
Bruno Munari, Italy

46
Cartoon
'The Tattooed Sailor'
André François, France

47
Illustration (Jazz)
Queen Magazine
Fletcher/Forbes/Gill, UK

48
Magazine Cover
Architectural &
Engineering News
Robert Brownjohn,
Tony Palladino, USA

49
Anonymous

50
Poster
France d'Aujourdhui
Gottlieb Soland,
Switzerland

51
Booklet Covers
Time Life Promotion
Louis Peace Klein, USA

52
Magazine Advertisement
Suddler &
Hennessy, Inc.
Herb Lubalin, USA

53
Trademark
Schwitter A.G.
Gerstner+Kutter,
Switzerland

54
Children's Book
Illustration
'I Know a Lot of
Things'
Paul Rand, USA

55
Magazine Cover
Theatre Arts
R.O. Blechman, USA

56
Book Jacket
Tony Palladino, USA

57
Booklet Cover
Cape Building
Products, Ltd.
Fletcher/Forbes/Gill, UK

58
Newspaper
Advertisement
C.B.S. Television
Network
Louis Dorfsman, USA

59
Newspaper Advertisement
Bohn Duplicator
Company
Herb Lubalin,
Dick Eskilson, USA

60
Poster
Gillette Safety Razor Co.
André François, France

61
Bus Poster
Pirelli Ltd.
Fletcher/Forbes/Gill, UK

62
Book Jacket
Dutton Paper Backs
Milton Glaser, USA

63
Trademark
C.B.S. Television
Network
William Golden, USA

64
Newspaper
Advertisement
Israel Airlines
Robert Levinson
Sidney Meyers, USA

65
Poster
The Times
Abram Games, UK

66
Illustration
Bok, 1956-59
Dieter Rot, Iceland

67
Series of Posters
Swedish Modern Museum
Melin & Österlin, Sweden

68
Poster
Moins de Bruit
Müller-Brockman,
Switzerland

69
Film Trademark
Bonjour Tristesse
Saul Bass, USA

70
Newspaper
Advertisement
Bergdoff Goodman Shoes
Reba Sochis, USA

71
Booklet Cover
I.B.M.
Charles Keddie, USA

72
Booklet Cover
Life International
Fletcher/Forbes/Gill, UK

73
Annual Report Cover
Pepsi-Cola Company
Brownjohn, Chermayeff
& Geismer, USA

74
Booklet Cover
N.Y. Life Insurance Co.
Herb Lubalin, USA

75
Magazine Advertisement
Woman's Day
Gene Federicko, USA

76
Magazine Advertisement
L+C
Heiniger, Müller
Brockmann, Switzerland

77
Magazine Advertisement
Exhibition of Textiles
Franco Grignani, Italy

78
Magazine Cover
Esquire
Henry Wolf, USA

79
Magazine Illustration
Esquire
Tomi Ungerer, USA

80
Page from Booklet
The Composing Room
Brownjohn, Chermayeff
& Geismar, USA

81
Trademark
Friederichs Heyking
(Steel)
Anton Stankowski,
Germany

82
Booklet Cover
W.C.B.S. Television
Irving Miller, USA

83
Announcement
Fletcher/Forbes/Gill, UK

84
Cartoon
'The Eye of the Needle'
John Glasham, UK

85
Magazine Cartoon
Town
Hans Haem, UK

86
Poster
Albert Landry Galleries
Georgy Tscherny, USA

87
Christmas Card
Fletcher/Forbes/Gill, UK

88
Booklet Cover
New York Times
Louis Silverstein, USA

89
Magazine Cover
I.C.I. Ltd. Plastics
Division
Colin Forbes, UK

90
Magazine Advertiseme
Sudler & Hennessy, Ir
Herb Lubalin, USA

91
Magazine Advertiseme
Coldene
George Lois, USA

92
Trademark
Electrical Products
Manufacturer
F. H. K. Henrion, UK

93
Trademark
Bech Electronic Centr
Gerstner+Kutter,
Switzerland

94
Film End Titles
West Side Story
Saul Bass, USA

We would like to than
all the above
contributors for their
kindness in allowing u
to reproduce their wo
We would also like to
thank Beatrix Miller a
Lila Karp for editorial
assistance.

Photo on back cover
by Michael Joseph